# SONGS *of* DEMOCRACY

*By*

WALT WHITMAN

### THICK-SPRINKLED BUNTING

*Thick-sprinkled bunting! Flag of stars!*
*Long yet your road, fateful flag!—long yet your road, and lined with*
*bloody death!*
*For the prize I see at issue, at last is the world!*
*All its ships and shores I see, interwoven with your threads, greedy banner!*
*—Dream'd again the flags of kings, highest born, to flaunt unrival'd?*
*O hasten, flag of man! O with sure and steady step, passing highest flags*
*of kings,*
*Walk supreme to the heavens, mighty symbol—run up above them all,*
*Flag of stars! thick-sprinkled bunting!*

PHILADELPHIA

DAVID McKAY, PUBLISHER

604–608 SOUTH WASHINGTON SQUARE

WINDHAM PRESS
CLASSIC REPRINTS

*Shut not your doors to me, proud libraries,*
*For that which was lacking on all your well-fill'd*
*  shelves, yet needed most, I bring;*
*Forth from the army, the war emerging—a book I*
*  have made,*
*The words of my book nothing—the drift of it every-*
*  thing;*
*A book separate, not link'd with the rest, nor felt by*
*  the intellect,*
*But you, ye untold latencies, will thrill to every page;*
*Through Space and Time fused in a chant, and the*
*  flowing, eternal Identity,*
*To Nature, encompassing these, encompassing God—*
*  to the joyous, electric All,*
*To the sense of Death—and accepting, exulting in*
*  Death, in its turn, the same as life,*
*The entrance of Man I sing.*

# INTRODUCTION

THOSE who know their Whitman will no doubt find somewhat ridiculous an enterprise which purposes to isolate a limited number of his poems under the title of the present volume, so completely is his work given up to the celebration of democracy. They will be fortified in their views, moreover, by the consciousness that the author himself would have shared them. Whitman saw in *Leaves of Grass* an organism, something which must be taken entire or not at all. Of the considerable number of "Selections" offered to the fearful, only two or three were published with his consent, and that a very reluctant consent, yielded at the promptings of a kindly desire not to wound with a rebuff the good intentions of his friends. He seems to have felt they were, after all, Edmund Clarence Stedman's or Elizabeth Porter Gould's selections, and as such were important only for the light they threw on the judgment of those excellent persons and the taste of their friends. He himself stood squarely by all that he had written, and refused to delete a line even at the urging of his much-admired Emerson. In his old age, face to face with his unpopularity, with the disapproval, even with the "anger and contempt," of his own time, he notes as "the best comfort of the whole business (after a band of the dearest friends and upholders ever vouchsafed to man or cause—doubtless all the more faithful and uncompromising —this little phalanx!—for being so few)" that "unstopp'd and unwarp'd by any influence outside the soul within me, I have had my say entirely my own way and put it unerringly on record—the value

thereof to be decided by time." Clearly it behooves
one who performs yet another mutilation to prove it
justified by different motives and conditions from
those upon which the poet passed when he registered
his veto.

Let it be understood, then, at the outset, that I
heartily sympathize with Whitman's attitude. I
have made no attempt to propitiate the self-ap-
pointed arbiters of "the best that is known and
thought in the world" by selecting those poems
which seem least scornful of the time-honored poetic
forms. There is not perhaps the same temptation
that once there was. The professors and critics,
judicially enthroned in their studies, handing down
decisions based on laws they derive from the tradi-
tions of the great dead, seldom keep in contact with
life, and life avenges itself by making a mulch of their
opinions to nourish the roots of future revolution-
aries, and by blinding their eyes to the secret of all
that is imperishable in literature. They cannot
answer in the affirmative Whitman's question, "Are
you done with reviews and criticisms of life? animat-
ing now to life itself?" hence they fail to see what he
sees so plainly, namely, that the greatest poet does
not court beauty, but that beauty follows him and
is faithful to him in proportion as he is successful in
interpreting the truth of his days and in auguring
from it the truth of the future; that beauty is eternal,
but that it grows and changes with the generations
as "truth grows by truth's addition." The best that
is known and thought in the world thus always eludes
them. Fitzgerald's "This will never do," echoed by
critics of Whitman, has become a formidable weapon
in the hands of modern poets. College professors,
discoursing oracularly upon the fundamental laws of
good poetry, still point out that, according to them,
Whitman is no poet, while the vers librists recognize

in him the author of their being. By this it is not
meant to imply that he has founded a school of men
who write as he does; in such a consummation he
would have seen the failure of his gospel, it being far
from his desire to become in his turn part of an
inflexible tradition which should cage the fancy of
the next generation,

"I charge that there be no theory or school founded out
    of me
  I charge that you leave all free as I have left all free."

He wished to establish the fact that forms must wait
upon reality, and that the stupendous expansion of
the modern world, especially that most stupendous
and modern part of it, America, had long outgrown
the ancestral stays of feudal poetry. Time has
approved his judgment. Today Masefield points to
the necessity for new forms, Galsworthy cries out
for some one to express "this amazing America,"
and American youth answers, "hear! hear!"

But if time is eliminating one cause of the numer-
ous "selected" editions, it has made little impres-
sion upon the more important one. We are still too
much under the influence of the medieval concep-
tion that the flesh is of the devil; of the actions
and reactions consequent on alternating clerical
asceticism and license, to have a sane, natural atti-
tude toward sex. It is no doubt for this reason that
Swinburne's *Poems and Ballads*, in which sex is
degraded to the sterility of mere sensation, is read in
homes and classrooms where *Leaves of Grass* is taboo.
It is not, however, from sympathy with the pre-
judices of those who believe the mechanism for prop-
agating human life essential, but essentially shame-
ful, that the so-called objectional poems are omitted
from this edition, but because its reason for being is
to show how truly Whitman is the poet of the hour,

9

how infinitely better than any of his countrymen
before or since his time he has expressed "this
amazing America," and because in this matter of a
dignified, wholesome, and moral attitude toward sex
—an attitude which does not look upon it primarily
as prolific of sensation, but rather in its relation to
parenthood, to the creation of fine types of men and
women—America has not yet grown up to Walt
Whitman.

These reasons only partly explain, however, why
"The Good Gray Poet" has been so long reaching the
audience for which he wrote, namely, "the common
average man." Other circumstances, inherent for
the most part in the conditions of his day, added
their weight to the general negation. They seem to
have centered, so far as such a tangle of causes and ef-
fects may be said to center, in the antagonism of "the
merely literary." Whitman himself had a cordial
contempt for the dicta of this group, but there is no
disputing its influence. For, paradoxical as it may
at first sight seem, the nation which even then was
producing the famous man from Missouri had no
confidence whatever in its literary judgment. There
was, of course, an excellent reason for this apparent
lack of mental independence. Average Americans,
displaying all the good sense Whitman credited
them with, were applying themselves with praise-
worthy singleness of mind to those tasks which he
insisted were preëminently the tasks of their age.

"Here first the duties of today, the lessons of the con-
        crete,
    Wealth, order, travel, shelter, products, plenty;
    As of the building of some varied, vast, perpetual
        edifice
    Whence to arise inevitable in time, the towering roofs,
        the lamps,
    The solid-planted spires tall shooting to the stars."

Literature was a secondary consideration, and, like the sensible men they were, they took the word of the specialists for the problems of their own field.

Unfortunately, the very conditions which underlay the attitude of the average man made the specialist unreliable. America furnished no exception to the rule that the greatest imaginations are normally attracted to the greatest need. The minds undertaking to determine the present and direct the future of her letters, compared with those undertaking to lay the foundations of her empire, were picayune; inferior in confidence and courage, in initiative and creative power. Far from recognizing the significance of the tremendous processes going on about them, they saw only the ugliness of their superficial manifestations. In the nature of things a small group, isolated by their conscious refinements, they held themselves superior to the world with which an unkind fate identified them, and apologetic, explanatory, they groveled at the feet of Europe. This tendency of America's men of letters to look upon her as an adjunct of their personalities was sometimes subtle, as in Lowell's case, sometimes unconscious, as in Emerson's, but it was unmistakable and persists in our own day, when it has attained its most complete expression in the works of Henry James. In Walt Whitman, with his uncompromising faith in his own land and his own days, with his unswerving belief in America's future and his complete repudiation of those who proposed to speak for her but who spoke with the voice of Europe, such men could find only one thing more to explain.

But gradually, as one by one we have been learning the lessons of the concrete; as the margin of wealth in the United States has increased, and with it leisure and the opportunity for reading and study; as labor has won with shorter hours and higher pay

the extension of the public school system, and as
higher education has become more general among the
middle classes, our criticism has begun to show a
different spirit, and the cloud of ignorance and pre-
judice which has obscured the value of *Leaves of
Grass* and militated against its being accorded its
rightful place in our literature, has begun to lift. It
is lifting very slowly, however. For though our
educational system is constantly growing and im-
proving, it is still superficial, haphazard, and inade-
quate. The emphasis of our courses in literature,
intermediate and collegiate, is still on the thing that
is said of a text rather than on the text itself, so that
the influence of the "merely literary" is still con-
siderable.

Yet even in this quarter there has been a certain
softening. "The swarm of reflectors and the polite"
have grown less vociferous as they realized, through
indisputable evidence of his influence on the most
important of modern French and English poets, that
Europe's interest in Whitman had its origin in his
work *per se*, and not, as they had anxiously feared, in
the index it might be supposed to furnish of the
character of materialistic, uncouth, and barbarian
America. But the degree of their mollification has
been conditioned by the extent to which these poets
have accepted his ideas, and this, naturally enough,
has been limited. The brilliant group which launched
the *Mercure de France* into fame was as firmly con-
vinced as was Whitman of the truth of Herder's
admonition to Goethe, that "really great poetry is
the result of a national spirit," hence the substance
of Whitman's poetry, grown out of American condi-
tions, and addressed as it was especially to Ameri-
cans, could have little influence on their work. His
*ars poetica* was a different matter. The genius of
the modern, the spirit of change, had been working

only less miraculously in western Europe than in America, and of all the old world countries France had perhaps greatest spiritual need of new forms. At any rate, her poets early saw the adaptability to their own conditions of a creed of literary individualism which owned but a single canon, namely, truth to one's world and one's reactions to it. In this form Whitman's influence crossed the channel to England and now, with all the respectability attendant upon a successful foreign appearance and a slight foreign accent, is coming back to us in the work of symbolists, imagists, vers librists, and other moderns. All of which "the merely literary" are pondering, with the result already intimated.

But Whitman's liberation of poetic form was only part, and a very small part, of his gift to his country. His great service was to evoke a principle of unity from the heterogeneity of racial and sectional interests that made up the America of his day and inform it with that emotion in the absence of which a national spirit may not be said to exist. So far the moderns have not followed him. Many, it is true, among them Edgar Lee Masters, Edwin Arlington Robinson, and Robert Frost, have gone to the American life they know for their material and their inspiration. But the America they know is limited. It is New England, or it is the Middle West, and the underlying tone is the tone of these sections, never the cosmic emotion that underlies, for example, the *Song of the Redwood Tree*.

It is interesting to see an ultra-modern group definitely excluding the cosmic poet. One of the rules the imagists have laid down for themselves is:

"To present an image (hence the name: 'Imagist').

"We are not a school of painters, but we believe that poetry should render particulars exactly and not deal in vague generalities, however magnificent and sonorous. It is for this reason that we oppose the cosmic poet, who seems to us to shirk the real difficulties of his art." Miss Amy Lowell elucidates by pointing out that the image need not be of an object or of a series of objects, but may be of so intangible a thing as a mood. All very well. But suppose the poet's mood rises above his hearth-stone, wings its way to the stars, and returns to brood warmly over the whole world; suppose his mood becomes cosmic; what then?

The imagists evidently evade the difficulty by evading the mood. At any rate, it is precisely the absence of such impulses that makes modern American poets, with all the beauty and promise of their work, disappointing to lovers of Whitman. To be an American was to him synonymous with the possession of cosmic consciousness, although he saw clearly enough that that consciousness was as yet potential. The poet's was the great privilege of giving it form and voice, making it actual.

"He supplies what wants supplying  . . .
. . . . . . . . . . . . . . . .
As he sees the farthest, he has the most faith,
His thoughts are the hymns of the praise of things."

America has been growing ever more diverse since Whitman's day, but recent events have proved its principle of unity as strong, if almost as unconscious, as when he first enunciated it. The great war has forced its intellectual recognition; when from this is born the need of its emotional expression Walt Whitman must come into his own. That eventuality would seem to be imminent. Meanwhile—

A recent review notices the adventures of one Mr. Bert Love, of St. Louis, described as a lonely Whitmanite whose "soul was questing for a chum in

Whitmanic camaraderie." Boston, having proved
itself innocent of any real understanding of "the
poetry of barbarism," he "sought in the editorial
sanctums of New York, as well as on the coast of
Bohemia that skirts the famous confines of Green-
wich village," but sought in vain. The editors
condemned Whitman for his immorality and his
"sex-stuff," apparently oblivious of the rest of his
work; the Bohemians were equally unsatisfactory
because, we infer, they admired him almost exclu-
sively for the same reason, "though they claimed to
hold his memory embalmed," and the disappointed
pilgrim gave up in despair when he was driven to the
basement bar "to drink in protest of the drivel
offered by some of the 'devotees' " at the Whitman
Fellowship dinner. Even in that sacred circle he had
felt himself alone save for the gentle ghost of an old
New England lady, the sole person beside himself
who had acquired the proper taste for Whitman,
which is like a taste neither for olives, for caviare, nor
for limburger, but for "orbit swinging stars, and for
milky-ways, and for infinitude unventured."

Mr. Love, no doubt, has been pleased to exaggerate
for the sake of emphasis. He is by no means as
solitary as he would have us believe. Nevertheless,
there is truth in what he says, for if one of New
York's foremost newspapers urged the other day
that Whitman's centenary be "worthily marked and
celebrated," and suggested tentatively that "in con-
sideration of the wide and powerful influence he has
exerted, and of the honor that should be paid in the
hour of democracy's triumph to the greatest poet of
democracy, his centenary is more deserving of cele-
bration than was that of James Russell Lowell," a
leading Philadelphia daily almost simultaneously put
the weight of its editorial columns behind the solemn
statement that not only was Whitman not a great

poet, but he was not a poet at all since his subjects were unsuitable even for prose! Unfortunately, though Whitman's reputation and prestige have been growing steadily, those to whom his name means nothing are still legion, those who talk glibly about him without having read a line of his work are a sufficiently large company, while those who talk from half knowledge are about as numerous and twice as mischievous.

The Philadelphia editor added his brick to the wall designed to keep Whitman from his public. Yet had he been conversant with the subject of his remarks, he could hardly have condemned as unfit for prose the selfsame subject the expression of which, by President Wilson, he had been waxing dithyrambic over during the past four years. For it is in these famous documents that the extent to which time has justified *Leaves of Grass* can most easily be measured. In his explanation of American phenomena, in his definition of American ideals, in his demand for open diplomacy and finally in his advocacy of a league of nations, Woodrow Wilson is but voicing with the calm knowledge of present support what Walt Whitman prophesied nearly fifty years ago with the passionate conviction of hope and belief. The most cursory survey of the works of both men reveals a startling number of parallel passages, which the few following will serve to illustrate:

*"America is a name which sounds in the ears of men everywhere as a synonym with individual opportunity because a synonym with individual liberty."—Woodrow Wilson.*

"The American compact is altogether with individuals. The only government is that which makes minute of individuals."—*Walt Whitman.*

# INTRODUCTION

*"Washington and his associates, like the barons at Runnymede, spoke and acted, not for a class, but for a people. It has been left for us to see to it that it shall be understood that they spoke and acted, not for a single people only, but for all mankind."*—Woodrow Wilson.

"Thou, Washington, art all the world's, the continents'
    entire—not yours alone America,
\*   \*   \*   \*   \*   \*   \*   \*   \*   \*   \*   \*   \*   \*
Wherever Freedom, poised by Toleration, swayed by law
Stands or is rising thy true monument."—*Walt Whitman.*

*"I summon you to comradeship."*—Woodrow Wilson.

"I will write the evangel poem of comrades."
               —*Walt Whitman.*

Whatever may be the verdict of history upon the grade of Mr. Wilson's statesmanship of this we may be sure even today: he is a successful politician. There are those who say he has his head in the clouds, but there are more who contend that if this is so he succeeds in performing at the same time the difficult exploit of keeping his ear to the ground. With a few notable exceptions he has spoken the convictions of that average man in whom Whitman saw the salvation of America and "at last the world."

In selecting these poems, while I have sought always to emphasize those giving most vivid expression to the ideas with which the consciousness of the world today is burning, I have tried to keep the organism of *Leaves of Grass* intact. That is to say, while I have, for the reasons before stated, omitted the poems devoted specifically to sex, and have reluctantly omitted, too, the magnificent treatments of death, the touching poems based on incidents of the Civil War, and certain others, as tending to blur the phase selected for presentation, the poems included leave no part of Whitman's position unstated.

The principle determining the arrangement was similar; that is, as little violence as possible has been done the sequence of ideas. Those poems in which the poet presents his credentials, so to speak, orients himself in his material and spiritual world, are followed by a group embodying the general philosophical basis for his conception of democracy and his belief in it, and these, first by the poems devoted more particularly to America, and then by those more particularly to other nations and to America's relation to them. At the end are a few of those Songs of Parting which show democracy's poet as serenely confident in the face of approaching death as he had been in the health and pride of a superb maturity that the scheme of things was finally good,

> "In this broad earth of ours,
> Amid the measureless grossness and the slag,
> Enclosed and safe within its central heart
> Nestles the seed Perfection."

and that, therefore, all the incidents of the Real tending to the Ideal, passing evil and death itself, would be found ultimately justified in time.   Seeing, as he did, "the scheme's culmination" in America, his last poem addressed to her characteristically advises a confident constructive optimism which we have need of today as never before.

"One song, America, before I go,
  I'd sing o'er all the rest with trumpet sound,
  For Thee—the Future.
  *  *  *  *  *  *  *  *  *  *  *  *  *  *  *  *
  Belief I sing—and Preparation;
  As Life and Nature are not great with reference to the
        Present only,
  But greater still from what is yet to come,
  Out of that formula for Thee I sing."

—B. M.

18

## I WAS LOOKING A LONG WHILE

I WAS looking a long while for a clue to the history
of the past for myself, and for these chants—and
now I have found it;
It is not in those paged fables in the libraries, (them I
neither accept nor reject;)
It is no more in the legends than in all else;
It is in the present—it is this earth to-day;
It is in Democracy—(the purport and aim of all the
past;)
It is the life of one man or one woman to-day—the
average man of to-day;
It is in languages, social customs, literatures, arts;
It is in the broad show of artificial things, ships,
machinery, politics, creeds, modern improvements,
and the interchange of nations,
All for the average man of to-day.


## ONE'S-SELF I SING

ONE'S-SELF I sing—a simple, separate Person;
Yet utter the word Democratic, the word
*En-masse.*

Of Physiology from top to toe I sing;
Not physiognomy alone, nor brain alone, is worthy
for the muse—I say the Form complete is worthier
far;
The Female equally with the male I sing.

Of Life immense in passion, pulse, and power,
Cheerful—for freest action form'd, under the laws
divine,
The Modern Man I sing.

## STARTING FROM PAUMANOK

### 1

STARTING from fish-shape Paumanok, where I
was born,
Well-begotten, and rais'd by a perfect mother;
After roaming many lands—lover of populous pave-
ments;
Dweller in Mannahatta, my city—or on southern
savannas;
Or a soldier camp'd, or carrying my knapsack and
gun—or a miner in California;
Or rude in my home in Dakota's woods, my diet
meat, my drink from the spring;
Or withdrawn to muse and meditate in some deep
recess,
Far from the clank of crowds, intervals passing, rapt
and happy;
Aware of the fresh free giver, the flowing Missouri—
aware of mighty Niagara;
Aware of the buffalo herds, grazing the plains—the
hirsute and strong-breasted bull;
Of earth, rocks, Fifth-month flowers, experienced—
stars, rain, snow, my amaze;
Having studied the mocking-bird's tones, and the
mountain-hawk's,
And heard at dusk the unrival'd one, the hermit
thrush from the swamp-cedars,
Solitary, singing in the West, I strike up for a New
World.

### 2

Victory, union, faith, identity, time,
The indissoluble compacts, riches, mystery,
Eternal progress, the kosmos, and the modern re-
ports.

This, then, is life;
Here is what has come to the surface after so many
    throes and convulsions.
How curious! how real!
Underfoot the divine soil—overhead the sun.

See, revolving, the globe;
The ancestor-continents, away, group'd together;
The present and future continents, north and south,
    with the isthmus between.

See, vast, trackless spaces;
As in a dream, they change, they swiftly fill;
Countless masses debouch upon them;
They are now cover'd with the foremost people, arts,
    institutions, known.

See, projected, through time,
For me, an audience interminable.

With firm and regular step they wend—they never
    stop,
Successions of men, Americanos, a hundred millions;
One generation playing its part, and passing on;
Another generation playing its part, and passing on
    in its turn,
With faces turn'd sideways or backward towards me,
    to listen,
With eyes retrospective towards me.

3

Americanos! conquerors! marches humanitarian;
Foremost! century marches! Libertad! masses!
For you a programme of chants.

Chants of the prairies;
Chants of the long-running Mississippi, and down
    to the Mexican sea;
Chants of Ohio, Indiana, Illinois, Iowa, Wisconsin
    and Minnesota;
Chants going forth from the centre, from Kansas,
    and thence, equi-distant,
Shooting in pulses of fire, ceaseless, to vivify all.


4

In the Year 80 of The States,
My tongue, every atom of my blood, form'd from
    this soil, this air,
Born here of parents born here, from parents the
    same, and their parents the same,
I, now thirty-six years old, in perfect health, begin,
Hoping to cease not till death.


Creeds and schools in abeyance,
(Retiring back a while, sufficed at what they are,
    but never forgotten,)
I harbor, for good or bad—I permit to speak, at
    every hazard,
Nature now without check, with original energy.


5

Take my leaves, America! take them, South, and
    take them, North!
Make welcome for them everywhere, for they are
    your own offspring;
Surround them, East and West! for they would sur-
    round you;
And you precedents! connect lovingly with them,
    for they connect lovingly with you.

I conn'd old times;
I sat studying at the feet of the great masters:
Now, if eligible, O that the great masters might re-
    turn and study me!


In the name of These States, shall I scorn the antique?
Why These are the children of the antique, to
    justify it.

6

Dead poets, philosophs, priests,
Martyrs, artists, inventors, governments long since,
Language-shapers, on other shores,
Nations once powerful, now reduced, withdrawn,
    or desolate,
I dare not proceed till I respectfully credit what you
    have left, wafted hither:
I have perused it—own it is admirable, (moving
    awhile among it;)
Think nothing can ever be greater—nothing can
    ever deserve more than it deserves;
Regarding it all intently a long while—then dismis-
    sing it,
I stand in my place, with my own day, here.


Here lands female and male;
Here the heir-ship and heiress-ship of the world—
    here the flame of materials;
Here Spirituality, the translatress, the openly-
    avow'd,
The ever-tending, the finale of visible forms;
The satisfier, after due long-waiting, now advancing,
Yes, here comes my mistress, the Soul.

7

The Soul:
Forever and forever—longer than soil is brown and
    solid—longer than water ebbs and flows.

I will make the poems of materials, for I think they
    are to be the most spiritual poems;
And I will make the poems of my body and of mor-
    tality,
For I think I shall then supply myself with the poems
    of my Soul, and of immortality.

I will make a song for These States, that no one
    State may under any circumstances be subjected
    to another State;
And I will make a song that there shall be comity
    by day and by night between all The States, and
    between any two of them:

And I will make a song for the ears of the President,
    full of weapons with menacing points,
And behind the weapons countless dissatisfied faces:
—And a song make I, of the One form'd out of all;
The fang'd and glittering One whose head is over
    all;
Resolute, warlike One, including and over all;
(However high the head of any else, that head is
    over all.)

I will acknowledge contemporary lands;
I will trail the whole geography of the globe, and
    salute courteously every city large and small;
And employments! I will put in my poems, that
    with you is heroism, upon land and sea;
And I will report all heroism from an American
    point of view.

I will sing the song of companionship;
I will show what alone must finally compact These;
I believe These are to found their own ideal of manly
    love, indicating it in me;
I will therefore let flame from me the burning fires
    that were threatening to consume me;
I will lift what has too long kept down those smoul-
    dering fires;
I will give them complete abandonment;
I will write the evangel-poem of comrades, and of
    love;
(For who but I should understand love, with all its
    sorrow and joy?
And who but I should be the poet of comrades?)


8

I am the credulous man of qualities, ages, races;
I advance from the people in their own spirit;
Here is what sings unrestricted faith.


Omnes! Omnes! let others ignore what they may;
I make the poem of evil also—I commemorate that
    part also;
I am myself just as much evil as good, and my nation
    is—And I say there is in fact no evil;
(Or if there is, I say it is just as important to you,
    to the land, or to me, as anything else.)


I too, following many, and follow'd by many, inaugu-
    rate a Religion—I descend into the arena;
(It may be I am destin'd to utter the loudest cries
    there, the winner's pealing shouts;
Who knows? they may rise from me yet, and soar
    above every thing.)

Each is not for its own sake;
I say the whole earth, and all the stars in the sky,
   are for Religion's sake.

I say no man has ever yet been half devout enough;
None has ever yet adored or worship'd half enough;
None has begun to think how divine he himself is,
   and how certain the future is.

I say that the real and permanent grandeur of These
   States must be their Religion;
Otherwise there is no real and permanent grandeur;
(Nor character, nor life worthy the name, without
   Religion;
Nor land, nor man or woman, without Religion.)


9

What are you doing, young man?
Are you so earnest—so given up to literature, science,
   art, amours?
These ostensible realities, politics, points?
Your ambition or business, whatever it may be?

It is well—Against such I say not a word—I am
   their poet also;
But behold! such swiftly subside—burnt up for Re-
   ligion's sake;
For not all matter is fuel to heat, impalpable flame,
   the essential life of the earth,
Any more than such are to Religion.


10

What do you seek, so pensive and silent?
What do you need, Camerado?
Dear son! do you think it is love?

Listen, dear son—listen, America, daughter or son!
It is a painful thing to love a man or woman to
 excess—and yet it satisfies—it is great;
But there is something else very great—it makes the
 whole coincide;
It, magnificent, beyond materials, with continuous
 hands, sweeps and provides for all.

II

Know you! solely to drop in the earth the germs of
 a greater Religion,
The following chants, each for its kind, I sing.

My comrade!
For you, to share with me, two greatnesses—and a
 third one, rising inclusive and more resplendent,
The greatness of Love and Democracy—and the
 greatness of Religion.

Melange mine own! the unseen and the seen;
Mysterious ocean where the streams empty;
Prophetic spirit of materials shifting and flickering
 around me;
Living beings, identities, now doubtless near us, in
 the air, that we know not of;
Contact daily and hourly that will not release me;
These selecting—these, in hints, demanded of me.

Not he, with a daily kiss, onward from childhood
 kissing me,
Has winded and twisted around me that which holds
 me to him,
Any more than I am held to the heavens, to the
 spiritual world,
And to the identities of the Gods, my lovers, faith-
 ful and true,
After what they have done to me, suggesting themes.

27

O such themes! Equalities!
O amazement of things! O divine average!
O warblings under the sun—usher'd, as now, or at
    noon, or setting!
O strain, musical, flowing through ages—now reach-
    ing hither!
I take to your reckless and composite chords—I add
    to them, and cheerfully pass them forward.

12

As I have walk'd in Alabama my morning walk,
I have seen where the she-bird, the mocking-bird, sat
    on her nest in the briers, hatching her brood.

I have seen the he-bird also;
I have paused to hear him, near at hand, inflating
    his throat, and joyfully singing.

And while I paused, it came to me that what he really
    sang for was not there only,
Nor for his mate, nor himself only, nor all sent back
    by the echoes;
But subtle, clandestine, away beyond,
A charge transmitted, and gift occult, for those being
    born.

13

Democracy!
Near at hand to you a throat is now inflating itself
    and joyfully singing.

Ma femme!
For the brood beyond us and of us,
For those who belong here, and those to come,
I, exultant, to be ready for them, will now shake
    out carols stronger and haughtier than have ever
    yet been heard upon earth.

I will make the songs of passion, to give them their
way,
And your songs, outlaw'd offenders—for I scan you
with kindred eyes, and carry you with me the
same as any.

I will make the true poem of riches,
To earn for the body and the mind whatever ad-
heres, and goes forward, and is not dropt by death.

I will effuse egotism, and show it underlying all—and
I will be the bard of personality;
And I will show of male and female that either is
but the equal of the other;
And sexual organs and acts! do you concentrate in
me—for I am determin'd to tell you with cour-
ageous clear voice, to prove you illustrious;
And I will show that there is no imperfection in the
present—and can be none in the future;
And I will show that whatever happens to anybody,
it may be turn'd to beautiful results—and I will
show that nothing can happen more beautiful
than death;
And I will thread a thread through my poems that
time and events are compact,
And that all the things of the universe are perfect
miracles, each as profound as any.

I will not make poems with reference to parts;
But I will make leaves, poems, poemets, songs, says,
thoughts with reference to ensemble:
And I will not sing with reference to a day, but with
reference to all days;
And I will not make a poem, nor the least part of a
poem, but has reference to the Soul;
(Because, having look'd at the objects of the uni-
verse, I find there is no one, nor any particle of
one, but has reference to the Soul.)

29

14

Was somebody asking to see the Soul?
See! your own shape and countenance—persons, sub-
    stances, beasts, the trees, the running rivers, the
    rocks and sands.

All hold spiritual joys, and afterwards loosen them:
How can the real body ever die, and be buried?

Of your real body, and any man's or woman's real
    body,
Item for item, it will elude the hands of the corpse-
    cleaners, and pass to fitting spheres,
Carrying what has accrued to it from the moment of
    birth to the moment of death.

Not the types set up by the printer return their im-
    pression, the meaning, the main concern,
Any more than a man's substance and life, or a
    woman's substance and life, return in the body
    and the Soul,
Indifferently before death and after death.

Behold! the body includes and is the meaning, the
    main concern—and includes and is the Soul;
Whoever you are! how superb and how divine is
    your body, or any part of it.

15

Whoever you are! to you endless announcements.

Daughter of the lands, did you wait for your poet?
Did you wait for one with a flowing mouth and in-
    dicative hand?

Toward the male of The States, and toward the
female of The States,
Live words—words to the lands.

O the lands! interlink'd, food-yielding lands!

Land of coal and iron! Land of gold! Lands of cot-
ton, sugar, rice!
Land of wheat, beef, pork! Land of wool and hemp!
Land of the apple and grape!
Land of the pastoral plains, the grass-fields of the
world! Land of those sweet-air'd interminable
plateaus!
Land of the herd, the garden, the healthy house of
adobie!
Lands where the northwest Columbia winds, and
where the southwest Colorado winds!
Land of the eastern Chesapeake! Land of the Dela-
ware!
Land of Ontario, Erie, Huron, Michigan!
Land of the Old Thirteen! Massachusetts land!
Land of Vermont and Connecticut!
Land of the ocean shores! Land of sierras and peaks!
Land of boatmen and sailors! Fishermen's land!
Inextricable lands! the clutch'd together! the pas-
sionate ones!
The side by side! the elder and younger brothers!
the bony-limb'd!
The great women's land! the feminine! the expe-
rienced sisters and the inexperienced sisters!
Far breath'd land! Arctic braced! Mexican breez'd!
the diverse! the compact!
The Pennsylvanian! the Virginian! the double Caro-
linian!
O all and each well-loved by me! my intrepid na-
tions! O I at any rate include you all with per-
fect love!

I cannot be discharged from you! not from one, any
sooner than another!
O Death! O for all that, I am yet of you, unseen,
this hour, with irrepressible love,
Walking New England, a friend, a traveler,
Splashing my bare feet in the edge of the summer
ripples, on Paumanok's sands,
Crossing the prairies—dwelling again in Chicago—
dwelling in every town,
Observing shows, births, improvements, structures,
arts,
Listening to the orators and the oratresses in public
halls,
Of and through The States, as during life—each man
and woman my neighbor,
The Louisianian, the Georgian, as near to me, and I
as near to him and her,
The Mississippian and Arkansian yet with me—and
I yet with any of them;
Yet upon the plains west of the spinal river—yet in
my house of adobie,
Yet returning eastward—yet in the Sea-Side State,
or in Maryland,
Yet Kanadian, cheerily braving the winter—the
snow and ice welcome to me,
Yet a true son either of Maine, or of the Granite
State, or of the Narragansett Bay State, or of the
Empire State;
Yet sailing to other shores to annex the same—yet
welcoming every new brother;
Hereby applying these leaves to the new ones, from
the hour they unite with the old ones;
Coming among the new ones myself, to be their
companion and equal—coming personally to you
now;
Enjoining you to acts, characters, spectacles, with
me.

### 16

With me, with firm holding—yet haste, haste on.

For your life, adhere to me!
Of all the men of the earth, I only can unloose you
  and toughen you;
I may have to be persuaded many times before I
  consent to give myself really to you—but what of
  that?
Must not Nature be persuaded many times?

No dainty dolce affettuoso I;
Bearded, sun-burnt, gray-neck'd, forbidding, I have
  arrived,
To be wrestled with as I pass, for the solid prizes of
  the universe;
For such I afford whoever can persevere to win them.

### 17

On my way a moment I pause;
Here for you! and here for America!
Still the Present I raise aloft—Still the Future of
  The States I harbinge, glad and sublime;
And for the Past, I pronounce what the air holds of
  the red aborigines.

The red aborigines!
Leaving natural breaths, sounds of rain and winds,
  calls as of birds and animals in the woods, syllabled
  to us for names;
Okonee, Koosa, Ottawa, Monongahela, Sauk, Nat-
  chez, Chattahoochee, Kaqueta, Oronoco,
Wabash, Miami, Saginaw, Chippewa, Oshkosh,
  Walla-Walla;
Leaving such to The States, they melt, they depart,
  charging the water and the land with names.

3

18

O expanding and swift!  O henceforth,
Elements, breeds, adjustments, turbulent, quick,
    and audacious;
A world primal again—Vistas of glory, incessant and
    branching;
A new race, dominating previous ones, and grander
    far—with new contests,
New politics, new literatures and religions, new in-
    ventions and arts.


These! my voice announcing—I will sleep no more,
    but arise;
You oceans that have been calm within me! how I
    feel you, fathomless, stirring, preparing unpre-
    cedented waves and storms.


19

See! steamers steaming through my poems!
See, in my poems immigrants continually coming
    and landing;
See, in arriere, the wigwam, the trail, the hunter's
    hut, the flat-boat, the maize-leaf, the claim, the
    rude fence, and the backwoods village;
See, on the one side the Western Sea, and on the
    other the Eastern Sea, how they advance and
    retreat upon my poems, as upon their own shores.


See, pastures and forests in my poems—See, animals,
    wild and tame—See, beyond the Kanzas, countless
    herds of buffalo, feeding on short curly grass;
See, in my poems, cities, solid, vast, inland, with
    paved streets, with iron and stone edifices, cease-
    less vehicles, and commerce;

See, the many-cylinder'd steam printing-press—See,
    the electric telegraph, stretching across the Con-
    tinent, from the Western Sea to Manhattan;
See, through Atlantica's depths, pulses American,
    Europe reaching—pulses of Europe, duly return'd;
See, the strong and quick locomotive, as it departs,
    panting, blowing the steam-whistle;
See, ploughmen, ploughing farms—See, miners, dig-
    ging mines—See, the numberless factories;
See, mechanics, busy at their benches, with tools—
    See from among them, superior judges, philosophs,
    Presidents, emerge, drest in working dresses;
See, lounging through the shops and fields of The
    States, me, well-belov'd, close-held by day and
    night;
Hear the loud echoes of my songs there!  Read the
    hints come at last.

20

O Camerado close!
O you and me at last—and us two only.

O a word to clear one's path ahead endlessly!
O something extatic and undemonstrable!  O music
    wild!

O now I triumph—and you shall also;
O hand in hand—O wholesome pleasure—O one
    more desirer and lover!
O to haste, firm holding—to haste, haste on with me.

## GODS

### 1

THOUGHT of the Infinite—the All!
Be thou my God.

### 2

Lover Divine, and Perfect Comrade!
Waiting, content, invisible yet, but certain,
Be thou my God.

### 3

Thou—thou, the Ideal Man!
Fair, able, beautiful, content, and loving,
Complete in Body, and dilate in Spirit,
Be thou my God.

### 4

O Death—(for Life has served its turn;)
Opener and usher to the heavenly mansion!
Be thou my God.

### 5

Aught, aught, of mightiest, best, I see, conceive, or
know,
(To break the stagnant tie—thee, thee to free, O Soul,)
Be thou my God.

### 6

Or thee, Old Cause, when'er advancing;
All great Ideas, the races' aspirations,
All that exalts, releases thee, my Soul!
All heroisms, deeds of rapt enthusiasts,
Be ye my Gods!

### 7

Or Time and Space!
Or shape of Earth, divine and wondrous!
Or shape in I myself—or some fair shape, I, viewing,
worship,
Or lustrous orb of Sun, or star by night:
Be ye my Gods.

## THOUGHT

OF Equality—As if it harm'd me, giving others
the same chances and rights as myself—
As if it were not indispensable to my own
rights that others possess the same.

## FOR HIM I SING

FOR him I sing,
I raise the Present on the Past,
(As some perennial tree, out of its roots, the
present on the past:)
With time and space I him dilate—and fuse the
immortal laws,
To make himself, by them, the law unto himself.

## LAWS FOR CREATIONS

LAWS for Creations,
For strong artists and leaders—for fresh broods
of teachers, and perfect literats for America,
For noble savans, and coming musicians.

All must have reference to the ensemble of the world,
and the compact truth of the world;
There shall be no subject too pronounced—All works
shall illustrate the divine law of indirections.

What do you suppose Creation is?
What do you suppose will satisfy the Soul, except to
walk free, and own no superior?
What do you suppose I would intimate to you in a
hundred ways, but that man or woman is as good
as God?

And that there is no God any more divine than
  Yourself?
And that that is what the oldest and newest myths
  finally mean?
And that you or any one must approach Creations
  through such laws?


## ON THE BEACH AT NIGHT ALONE

ON the beach at night alone,
  As the old mother sways her to and fro, sing-
    ing her husky song,
As I watch the bright stars shining—I think a
  thought of the clef of the universes, and of the
  future.


A vast similitude interlocks all,
All spheres, grown, ungrown, small, large, suns,
  moons, planets, comets, asteroids,
All the substances of the same, and all that is spirit-
  ual upon the same,
All distances of place, however wide,
All distances of time—all inanimate forms,
All Souls—all living bodies, though they be ever so
  different, or in different worlds,
All gaseous, watery, vegetable, mineral processes—
  the fishes, the brutes,
All men and women—me also;
All nations, colors, barbarisms, civilizations, lan-
  guages;
All identities that have existed, or may exist, on this
  globe, or any globe;
All lives and deaths—all of the past, present, future;
This vast similitude spans them, and always has
  spann'd, and shall forever span them, and com-
  pactly hold them, and enclose them.

## SONG OF THE UNIVERSAL

### 1

COME, said the Muse,
Sing me a song no poet yet has chanted,
Sing me the Universal.

In this broad Earth of ours,
Amid the measureless grossness and the slag,
Enclosed and safe within its central heart,
Nestles the seed Perfection.

By every life a share, or more or less,
None born but it is born—conceal'd or unconceal'd,
    the seed is waiting.

### 2

Lo! keen-eyed, towering Science!
As from tall peaks the Modern overlooking,
Successive, absolute fiats issuing.

Yet again, lo! the Soul—above all science;
For it, has History gather'd like a husk around the
    globe;
For it, the entire star-myriads roll through the sky.

In spiral roads, by long detours,
(As a much-tacking ship upon the sea,)
For it, the partial to the permanent flowing,
For it, the Real to the Ideal tends.

For it, the mystic evolution;
Not the right only justified—what we call evil also
    justified.

Forth from their masks, no matter what,
From the huge, festering trunk—from craft and guile
   and tears,
Health to emerge, and joy—joy universal.

Out of the bulk, the morbid and the shallow,
Out of the bad majority—the varied, countless
   frauds of men and States,
Electric, antiseptic yet—cleaving, suffusing all,
Only the good is universal.

3

Over the mountain growths, disease and sorrow,
An uncaught bird is ever hovering, hovering,
High in the purer, happier air.

From imperfection's murkiest cloud,
Darts always forth one ray of perfect light,
One flash of Heaven's glory.

To fashion's, custom's discord,
To the mad Babel-din, the deafening orgies,
Soothing each lull, a strain is heard, just heard,
From some far shore, the final chorus sounding.

4

O the blest eyes! the happy hearts!
That see—that know the guiding thread so fine,
Along the mighty labyrinth!

5

And thou, America!
For the Scheme's culmination—its Thought, and its
   Reality,
For these, (not for thyself,) Thou hast arrived.

Thou too surroundest all;
Embracing, carrying, welcoming all, Thou too, by
    pathways broad and new,
To the Ideal tendest.

The measur'd faiths of other lands—the grandeurs of
    the past,
Are not for Thee—but grandeurs of Thine own;
Deific faiths and amplitudes, absorbing, compre-
    hending all,
All eligible to all.

All, all for Immortality!
Love, like the light, silently wrapping all!
Nature's amelioration blessing all!
The blossoms, fruits of ages—orchards divine and
    certain;
Forms, objects, growths, humanities, to spiritual
    Images ripening.

### 6

Give me, O God, to sing that thought!
Give me—give him or her I love, this quenchless
    faith
In Thy ensemble.  Whatever else withheld, withhold
    not from us,
Belief in plan of Thee enclosed in Time and Space;
Health, peace, salvation universal.

Is it a dream?
Nay, but the lack of it the dream,
And, failing it, life's lore and wealth a dream,
And all the world a dream.

## THINK OF THE SOUL

THINK of the Soul;
    I swear to you that body of yours gives pro-
        portions to your Soul somehow to live in
    other spheres;
I do not know how, but I know it is so.

Think of loving and being loved;
I swear to you, whoever you are, you can interfuse
    yourself with such things that everybody that sees
    you shall look longingly upon you.

Think of the past;
I warn you that in a little while others will find their
    past in you and your times.

The race is never separated—nor man nor woman
    escapes;
All is inextricable—things, spirits, Nature, nations,
    you too—from precedents you come.

Recall the ever-welcome defiers, (The mothers pre-
    cede them;)
Recall the sages, poets, saviors, inventors, lawgivers,
    of the earth;

Recall Christ, brother of rejected persons—brother
    of slaves, felons, idiots, and of insane and diseas'd
    persons.

Think of the time when you were not yet born;
Think of times you stood at the side of the dying;
Think of the time when your own body will be dying.

Think of spiritual results,
Sure as the earth swims through the heavens, does
   every one of its objects pass into spiritual results.

Think of manhood, and you to be a man;
Do you count manhood, and the sweet of manhood,
   nothing?

Think of womanhood, and you to be a woman;
The creation is womanhood;
Have I not said that womanhood involves all?
Have I not told how the universe has nothing better
   than the best womanhood?

## THE MYSTIC TRUMPETER

1

HARK! some wild trumpeter—some strange
      musician,
      Hovering unseen in air, vibrates capricious
tunes to-night.

I hear thee, trumpeter—listening, alert, I catch thy
   notes,
Now pouring, whirling like a tempest round me,
Now low, subdued—now in the distance lost.

2

Come nearer, bodiless one—haply, in thee resounds
Some dead composer—haply thy pensive life
Was fill'd with aspirations high—unform'd ideals,
Waves, oceans musical, chaotically surging,
That now, ecstatic ghost, close to me bending, thy
   cornet echoing, pealing,
Gives out to no one's ears but mine—but freely gives
   to mine,
That I may thee translate.

43

### 3

Blow, trumpeter, free and clear—I follow thee,
While at thy liquid prelude, glad, serene,
The fretting world, the streets, the noisy hours of
    day, withdraw;
A holy calm descends, like dew, upon me,
I walk, in cool refreshing night, the walks of Para-
    dise,
I scent the grass, the moist air, and the roses;
Thy song expands my numb'd, imbonded spirit—
    thou freest, launchest me,
Floating and basking upon Heaven's lake.

### 4

Blow again, trumpeter! and for my sensuous eyes,
Bring the old pageants—show the feudal world.

What charm thy music works!—thou makest pass
    before me,
Ladies and cavaliers long dead—barons are in their
    castle halls—the troubadours are singing;
Arm'd knights go forth to redress wrongs—some in
    quest of the Holy Grail:
I see the tournament—I see the contestants, encased
    in heavy armor, seated on stately, champing
    horses;
I hear the shouts—the sounds of blows and smiting
    steel:
I see the Crusaders' tumultuous armies—Hark! how
    the cymbals clang!
Lo! where the monks walk in advance, bearing the
    cross on high!

### 5

Blow again, trumpeter! and for thy theme,
Take now the enclosing theme of all—the solvent
    and the setting;

44

*Love,* that is pulse of all—the sustenance and the
  pang;
The heart of man and woman all for love;
No other theme but love—knitting, enclosing, all-
  diffusing love.


O, how the immortal phantoms crowd around me!
I see the vast alembic ever working—I see and know
  the flames that heat the world;
The glow, the blush, the beating hearts of lovers,
So blissful happy some—and some so silent, dark,
  and nigh to death:
Love, that is all the earth to lovers—Love, that
  mocks time and space;
Love, that is day and night—Love, that is sun and
  moon and stars;
Love, that is crimson, sumptuous, sick with per-
  fume;
No other words, but words of love—no other thought
  but Love.


6

Blow again, trumpeter—conjure war's wild alarums.
Swift to thy spell, a shuddering hum like distant
  thunder rolls;
Lo! where the arm'd men hasten—Lo! mid the clouds
  of dust, the glint of bayonets;
I see the grime-faced cannoniers—I mark the rosy
  flash amid the smoke—I hear the cracking of the
  guns:
—Nor war alone—thy fearful music-song, wild
  player, brings every sight of fear,
The deeds of ruthless brigands—rapine, murder—I
  hear the cries for help!
I see ships foundering at sea—I behold on deck, and
  below deck, the terrible tableaux.

7

O trumpeter! methinks I am myself the instrument
    thou playest!
Thou melt'st my heart, my brain—thou movest,
    drawest, changest them, at will:
And now thy sullen notes send darkness through me;
Thou takest away all cheering light—all hope:
I see the enslaved, the overthrown, the hurt, the
    opprest of the whole earth;
I feel the measureless shame and humiliation of my
    race—it becomes all mine;
Mine too the revenges of humanity—the wrongs of
    ages—baffled feuds and hatreds;
Utter defeat upon me weighs—all lost! the foe vic-
    torious!
(Yet 'mid the ruins Pride colossal stands, unshaken
    to the last;
Endurance, resolution, to the last.)


8

Now, trumpeter, for thy close,
Vouchsafe a higher strain than any yet;
Sing to my soul—renew its languishing faith and
    hope;
Rouse up my slow belief—give me some vision of the
    future;
Give me, for once, its prophecy and joy.


O glad, exulting, culminating song!
A vigor more than earth's is in thy notes!
Marches of victory—man disenthrall'd—the con-
    queror at last!
Hymns to the universal God, from universal Man—
    all joy!
A reborn race appears—a perfect World, all joy!

Women and Men, in wisdom, innocence and health—
    all joy!
Riotous, laughing bacchanals, fill'd with joy!
War, sorrow, suffering gone—The rank earth purged
    —nothing but joy left!
The ocean fill'd with joy—the atmosphere all joy!
Joy! Joy! in freedom, worship, love!  Joy in the
    ecstacy of life!
Enough to merely be! Enough to breathe!
Joy! Joy! all over Joy!


## TO HIM THAT WAS CRUCIFIED

MY spirit to yours, dear brother;
    Do not mind because many, sounding your
        name, do not understand you;
I do not sound your name, but I understand you,
    (there are others also;)
I specify you with joy, O my comrade, to salute you,
    and to salute those who are with you, before and
    since—and those to come also,
That we all labor together, transmitting the same
    charge and succession;
We few, equals, indifferent of lands, indifferent of
    times;
We, enclosers of all continents, all castes—allowers
    of all theologies,
Compassionaters, perceivers, rapport of men,
We walk silent among disputes and assertions, but
    reject not the disputers, nor any thing that is
    asserted;
We hear the bawling and din—we are reach'd at
    by divisions, jealousies, recriminations on every
    side,
They close peremptorily upon us, to surround us, my
    comrade,

47

Yet we walk unheld, free, the whole earth over,
   journeying up and down, till we make our in-
   effaceable mark upon time and the diverse eras,
Till we saturate time and eras, that the men and
   women of races, ages to come, may prove brethren
   and lovers, as we are.


## THE BASE OF ALL METAPHYSICS

AND now, gentlemen,
   A word I give to remain in your memories and
      minds,
As base, and finale too, for all metaphysics.

(So, to the students, the old professor,
At the close of his crowded course.)

Having studied the new and antique, the Greek and
   Germanic systems,
Kant having studied and stated—Fichte and Schell-
   ing and Hegel,
Stated the lore of Plato—and Socrates, greater than
   Plato,
And greater than Socrates sought and stated—
   Christ divine having studied long,
I see reminiscent to-day those Greek and Germanic
   systems,
See the philosophies all—Christian churches and
   tenets see,
Yet underneath Socrates clearly see—and under-
   neath Christ the divine I see,
The dear love of man for his comrade—the attraction
   of friend to friend,
Of the well-married husband and wife—of children
   and parents,
Of city for city, and land for land.

## I HEAR IT WAS CHARGED AGAINST ME

I HEAR it was charged against me that I sought
to destroy institutions;
But really I am neither for nor against institu-
tions;
(What indeed have I in common with them?—Or
what with the destruction of them?)
Only I will establish in the Mannahatta, and in every
city of These States, inland and seaboard,
And in the fields and woods, and above every keel,
little or large, that dents the water,
Without edifices, or rules, or trustees, or any argu-
ment,
The institution of the dear love of comrades.

## A SONG

### 1

COME, I will make the continent indissoluble;
I will make the most splendid race the sun
ever yet shone upon;
I will make divine magnetic lands,
With the love of comrades,
With the life-long love of comrades.

### 2

I will plant companionship thick as trees along all the
rivers of America, and along the shores of the great
lakes, and all over the prairies;
I will make inseparable cities, with their arms about
each other's necks;
By the love of comrades,
By the manly love of comrades.

4                    49

3

For you these, from me, O Democracy, to serve you,
ma femme!
For you! for you, I am trilling these songs,
In the love of comrades,
In the high-towering love of comrades.

## STATES!

STATES!
Were you looking to be held together by the
lawyers?
By an agreement on a paper?  Or by arms?

Away!
I arrive, bringing these, beyond all the forces of
courts and arms,
These! to hold you together as firmly as the earth
itself is held together.

The old breath of life, ever new,
Here! I pass it by contact to you, America.

O mother! have you done much for me?
Behold, there shall from me be much done for you.

There shall from me be a new friendship—It shall be
called after my name,
It shall circulate through The States, indifferent of
place,
It shall twist and intertwist them through and
around each other—Compact shall they be, show-
ing new signs,
Affection shall solve every one of the problems of
freedom,
Those who love each other shall be invincible,
They shall finally make America completely vic-
torious, in my name.

One from Massachusetts shall be comrade to a Missourian,
One from Maine or Vermont, and a Carolinian and
an Oregonese, shall be friends triune, more precious
to each other than all the riches of the earth.

To Michigan shall be wafted perfume from Florida,
To the Mannahatta from Cuba or Mexico,
Not the perfume of flowers, but sweeter, and wafted
beyond death.

No danger shall balk Columbia's lovers,
If need be, a thousand shall sternly immolate themselves for one,
The Kanuck shall be willing to lay down his life for
the Kansian, and the Kansian for the Kanuck, on
due need.

It shall be customary in all directions, in the houses
and streets, to see manly affection,
The departing brother or friend shall salute the remaining brother or friend with a kiss.

There shall be innovations,
There shall be countless linked hands—namely, the
Northeasterner's, and the Northwesterner's, and
the Southwesterner's, and those of the interior,
and all their brood,
These shall be masters of the world under a new
power,
They shall laugh to scorn the attacks of all the remainder of the world.

The most dauntless and rude shall touch face to face
lightly,
The dependence of Liberty shall be lovers,
The continuance of Equality shall be comrades.

51

These shall tie and band stronger than hoops of iron,
I, extatic, O partners! O lands! henceforth with the
love of lovers tie you.

## TO A HISTORIAN

YOU who celebrate bygones!
    Who have explored the outward, the surfaces
        of the races—the life that has exhibited itself;
Who have treated of man as the creature of politics,
    aggregates, rulers and priests;
I, habitan of the Alleghanies, treating of him as he
    is in himself, in his own rights,
Pressing the pulse of the life that has seldom ex-
    hibited itself, (the great pride of man in himself;)
Chanter of Personality, outlining what is yet to be,
I project the history of the future.

## STILL THOUGH THE ONE I SING

STILL, though the one I sing,
    (One, yet of contradictions made,) I dedicate to
        Nationality,
I leave in him Revolt, (O latent right of insurrection!
    O quenchless, indispensable fire!)

## THOUGHT

OF obedience, faith, adhesiveness;
    As I stand aloof and look, there is to me some-
        thing profoundly affecting in large masses
of men, following the lead of those who do not be-
lieve in men.

## WITH ANTECEDENTS

### 1

WITH antecedents;
  With my fathers and mothers, and the ac-
    cumulations of past ages;
With all which, had it not been, I would not now be
  here, as I am:
With Egypt, India, Phenicia, Greece and Rome;
With the Kelt, the Scandinavian, the Alb, and the
  Saxon;
With antique maritime ventures,—with laws, arti-
  zanship, wars and journeys;
With the poet, the skald, the saga, the myth, and
  the oracle;
With the sale of slaves—with enthusiasts—with the
  troubadour, the crusader, and the monk;
With those old continents whence we have come to
  this new continent;
With the fading kingdoms and kings over there;
With the fading religions and priests;
With the small shores we look back to from our own
  large and present shores;
With countless years drawing themselves onward,
  and arrived at these years;
You and Me arrived—America arrived, and making
  this year;
This year! sending itself ahead countless years to
  come.

### 2

O but it is not the years—it is I—it is You;
We touch all laws, and tally all antecedents;
We are the skald, the oracle, the monk, and the
  knight—we easily include them, and more;
We stand amid time, beginningless and endless—we
  stand amid evil and good;

53

All swings around us—there is as much darkness as
   light;
The very sun swings itself and its system of planets
   around us;
Its sun, and its again, all swing around us.

As for me, (torn, stormy, even as I, amid these vehe-
   ment days,)
I have the idea of all, and am all, and believe in all;
I believe materialism is true, and spiritualism is true
   —I reject no part.

Have I forgotten any part?
Come to me, whoever and whatever, till I give you
   recognition.

I respect Assyria, China, Teutonia, and the Hebrews;
I adopt each theory, myth, god, and demi-god;
I see that the old accounts, bibles, genealogies, are
   true, without exception;
I assert that all past days were what they should
   have been;
And that they could no-how have been better than
   they were,
And that to-day is what it should be—and that
   America is,
And that to-day and America could no-how be better
   than they are.

3

In the name of These States, and in your and my
   name, the Past,
And in the name of These States, and in your and my
   name, the Present time.

I know that the past was great, and the future will be
   great,
And I know that both curiously conjoint in the pres-
   ent time,

(For the sake of him I typify—for the common aver-
  age man's sake—your sake, if you are he;)
And that where I am, or you are, this present day,
  there is the centre of all days, all races,
And there is the meaning, to us, of all that has ever
  come of races and days, or ever will come.


## TO FOREIGN LANDS

I HEARD that you ask'd for something to prove
  this puzzle, the New World,
  And to define America, her athletic Democracy;
Therefore I send you my poems, that you behold in
  them what you wanted.

## AMERICA

*CENTRE of equal daughters, equal sons,*
    *All, all alike endear'd, grown, ungrown, young or*
      *old,*
*Strong, ample, fair, enduring, capable, rich,*
*Perennial with the Earth, with Freedom, Law and Love,*
*A grand, sane, towering, seated Mother,*
*Chair'd in the adamant of Time.*

## I HEAR AMERICA SINGING

I HEAR America singing, the varied carols I hear;
  Those of mechanics—each one singing his, as
  it should be, blithe and strong;
The carpenter singing his, as he measures his plank
  or beam,
The mason singing his, as he makes ready for work,
  or leaves off work;
The boatman singing what belongs to him in his
  boat—the deck-hand singing on the steamboat
  deck;
The shoemaker singing as he sits on his bench—the
  hatter singing as he stands;
The wood-cutter's song—the ploughboy's, on his
  way in the morning, or at the noon intermission,
  or at sundown;
The delicious singing of the mother—or of the young
  wife at work—or of the girl sewing or washing—
  Each singing what belongs to her, and to none else;
The day what belongs to the day—At night, the
  party of young fellows, robust, friendly,
Singing, with open mouths, their strong melodious
  songs.

## TO THE EAST AND TO THE WEST

TO the East and to the West;
  To the man of the Seaside State, and of Penn-
  sylvania,
To the Kanadian of the North—to the Southerner
  I love;
These, with perfect trust, to depict you as myself—
  the germs are in all men;
I believe the main purport of These States is to found
  a superb friendship, exalté, previously unknown,
Because I perceive it waits, and has been always
  waiting, latent in all men.

## THE PRAIRIE STATES

A NEWER garden of creation, no primal solitude,
　　Dense, joyous, modern, populous millions,
cities and farms,
With iron interlaced, composite, tied, many in one,
By all the world contributed—freedom's and law's
　　and thrift's society,
The crown and teeming paradise, so far, of time's
　　accumulations,
To justify the past.

## THE PRAIRIE-GRASS DIVIDING

THE prairie-grass dividing—its special odor
　　breathing,
　　I demand of it the spiritual corresponding,
Demand the most copious and close companionship
　　of men,
Demand the blades to rise of words, acts, beings,
Those of the open atmosphere, coarse, sunlit, fresh,
　　nutritious,
Those that go their own gait, erect, stepping with
　　freedom and command—leading, not following,
Those with a never-quell'd audacity—those with
　　sweet and lusty flesh, clear of taint,
Those that look carelessly in the faces of Presidents
　　and Governors, as to say, *Who are you?*
Those of earth-born passion, simple, never-constrain'd, never obedient,
Those of inland America.

## SONG OF THE REDWOOD-TREE

### 1

A CALIFORNIA song!
A prophecy and indirection—a thought impalpable, to breathe, as air;
A chorus of dryads, fading, departing—or hamadryads departing;
A murmuring, fateful, giant voice, out of the earth and sky,
Voice of a mighty dying tree in the Redwood forest dense.

*Farewell, my brethren,*
*Farewell, O earth and sky—farewell, ye neighboring*
   *waters;*
*My time has ended, my term has come.*

### 2

Along the northern coast,
Just back from the rock-bound shore, and the caves,
In the saline air from the sea, in the Mendocino country,
With the surge for bass and accompaniment low and hoarse,
With crackling blows of axes, sounding musically, driven by strong arms,
Riven deep by the sharp tongues of the axes—there in the Redwood forest dense,
I heard the mighty tree its death-chant chanting.

The choppers heard not—the camp shanties echoed not;
The quick-ear'd teamsters, and chain and jack-screw men, heard not,
As the wood-spirits came from their haunts of a thousand years, to join the refrain;
But in my soul I plainly heard.

Murmuring out of its myriad leaves,
Down from its lofty top, rising two hundred feet high,
Out of its stalwart trunk and limbs—out of its foot-
    thick bark,
That chant of the seasons and time—chant, not of
    the past only, but the future.


3

*You untold life of me,*
*And all you venerable and innocent joys,*
*Perennial, hardy life of me, with joys, 'mid rain, and*
    *many a summer sun,*
*And the white snows, and night, and the wild winds;*
*O the great patient, rugged joys! my soul's strong joys,*
    *unreck'd by man;*
*(For know I bear the soul befitting me—I too have con-*
    *sciousness, identity,*
*And all the rocks and mountains have—and all the*
    *earth;)*
*Joys of the life befitting me and brothers mine,*
*Our time, our term has come.*


*Nor yield we mournfully, majestic brothers,*
*We who have grandly fill'd our time;*
*With Nature's calm content, and tacit, huge delight,*
*We welcome what we wrought for through the past,*
*And leave the field for them.*


*For them predicted long,*
*For a superber Race—they too to grandly fill their time,*
*For them we abdicate—in them ourselves, ye forest*
    *kings!*
*In them these skies and airs—these mountain peaks—*
    *Shasta—Nevadas,*
*These huge, precipitous cliffs—this amplitude—these*
    *valleys grand—Yosemite,*
*To be in them absorb'd, assimilated.*

4

Then to a loftier strain,
Still prouder, more ecstatic, rose the chant,
As if the heirs, the Deities of the West,
Joining, with master-tongue, bore part.


*Not wan from Asia's fetishes,*
*Nor red from Europe's old dynastic slaughter-house,*
*(Area of murder-plots of thrones, with scent left yet of*
*    wars and scaffolds every where,)*
*But come from Nature's long and harmless throes—*
*    peacefully builded thence,*
*These virgin lands—Lands of the Western Shore,*
*To the new Culminating Man—to you, the Empire*
*    New.*
*You, promis'd long, we pledge, we dedicate.*


*You occult, deep volitions,*
*You average Spiritual Manhood, purpose of all, pois'd*
*    on yourself—giving, not taking law,*
*You Womanhood divine, mistress and source of all,*
*    whence life and love, and aught that comes from life*
*    and love,*
*You unseen Moral Essence of all the vast materials of*
*    America, (age upon age, working in Death the same*
*    as Life,)*
*You that, sometimes known, oftener unknown, really*
*    shape and mould the New World, adjusting it to*
*    Time and Space,*
*You hidden National Will, lying in your abysms, con-*
*    ceal'd, but ever alert,*
*You past and present purposes, tenaciously pursued,*
*    may-be unconscious of yourselves,*
*Unswerv'd by all the passing errors, perturbations of the*
*    surface;*

*You vital, universal, deathless germs, beneath all creeds,
    arts, statutes, literatures,*
*Here build your homes for good—establish here—These
    areas entire, Lands of the Western Shore,*
*We pledge, we dedicate to you.*


*For man of you—your characteristic Race,*
*Here may he hardy, sweet, gigantic grow—here tower,
    proportionate to Nature,*
*Here climb the vast, pure spaces, unconfined, uncheck'd
    by wall or roof,*
*Here laugh with storm or sun—here joy—here patiently
    inure,*
*Here heed himself, unfold himself (not others' formulas
    heed)—here fill his time,*
*To duly fall, to aid, unreck'd at last,*
*To disappear, to serve.*


Thus, on the northern coast,
In the echo of teamsters' calls, and the clinking
    chains, and the music of choppers' axes,
The falling trunk and limbs, the crash, the muffled
    shriek, the groan,
Such words combined from the Redwood-tree—as of
    wood-spirits' voices ecstatic, ancient and rustling,
The century-lasting, unseen dryads, singing, with-
    drawing,
All their recesses of forests and mountains leaving,
From the Cascade range to the Wasatch—or Idaho
    far, or Utah,
To the deities of the Modern henceforth yielding,
The chorus and indications, the vistas of coming
    humanity—the settlements, features all,
In the Mendocino woods I caught.

5

The flashing and golden pageant of California!
The sudden and gorgeous drama—the sunny and
    ample lands;
The long and varied stretch from Puget Sound to
    Colorado south;
Lands bathed in sweeter, rarer, healthier air—valleys
    and mountain cliffs;
The fields of Nature long prepared and fallow—the
    silent, cyclic chemistry;
The slow and steady ages plodding—the unoccupied
    surface ripening—the rich ores forming beneath;
At last the New arriving, assuming, taking posses-
    sion,
A swarming and busy race settling and organizing
    every where;
Ships coming in from the whole round world, and
    going out to the whole world,
To India and China and Australia, and the thousand
    island paradises of the Pacific;
Populous cities—the latest inventions—the steamers
    on the rivers –the railroads—with many a thrifty
    farm, with machinery,
And wool, and wheat, and the grape—and diggings
    of yellow gold.

6

But more in you than these, Lands of the Western
    Shore!
(These but the means, the implements, the standing-
    ground,)
I see in you, certain to come, the promise of thou-
    sands of years, till now deferr'd,
Promis'd, to be fulfill'd, our common kind, the
    Race.

The New Society at last, proportionate to Nature,
In Man of you, more than your mountain peaks,
    or stalwart trees imperial,
In Woman more, far more, than all your gold, or
    vines, or even vital air.


Fresh come, to a New World indeed, yet long pre-
    pared,
I see the Genius of the Modern, child of the Real and
    Ideal,
Clearing the ground for broad humanity, the true
    America, heir of the past so grand,
To build a grander future.


## POEM OF REMEMBRANCE FOR A GIRL OR
A BOY OF THESE STATES

YOU just maturing youth! You male or female!
    Remember the organic compact of These States,
    Remember the pledge of the Old Thirteen
thenceforward to the rights, life, liberty, equality
of man,
Remember what was promulged by the founders,
    ratified by The States, signed in black and white
    by the Commissioners, and read by Washington
    at the head of the army.
Remember the purposes of the founders,—Remem-
    ber Washington;
Remember the copious humanity streaming from
    every direction toward America;
Remember the hospitality that belongs to nations
    and men; (Cursed be nation, woman, man, with-
    out hospitality!)
Remember, government is to subserve individuals,

Not any, not the President, is to have one jot more
   than you or me,
Not any habitan of America is to have one jot less
   than you or me.

Anticipate when the thirty or fifty millions, are to
   become the hundred, or two hundred millions, of
   equal freemen and freewomen, amicably joined.

Recall ages—One age is but a part—ages are but a
   part;
Recall the angers, bickerings, delusions, supersti-
   tions, of the idea of caste,
Recall the bloody cruelties and crimes.

Anticipate the best women;
I say an unnumbered new race of hardy and well-de-
   fined women are to spread through all These
   States,
I say a girl fit for These States must be free, capable,
   dauntless, just the same as a boy.

Anticipate your own life—retract with merciless
   power,
Shirk nothing—retract in time—Do you see those
   errors, diseases, weaknesses, lies, thefts?
Do you see that lost character?—Do you see decay,
   consumption, rum-drinking, dropsy, fever, mortal
   cancer or inflammation?
Do you see death, and the approach of death?

5                  65

## AN OLD MAN'S THOUGHT OF SCHOOL

AN old man's thought of School;
　　An old man, gathering youthful memories and
　　　blooms, that youth itself cannot.

Now only do I know you!
O fair auroral skies!　O morning dew upon the grass!

And these I see—these sparkling eyes,
These stores of mystic meaning—these young lives,
Building, equipping, like a fleet of ships—immortal
　　ships!
Soon to sail out over the measureless seas,
On the Soul's voyage.

Only a lot of boys and girls?
Only the tiresome spelling, writing, ciphering classes?
Only a Public School?

Ah more—infinitely more;
(As George Fox rais'd his warning cry, "Is it this
　　pile of brick and mortar—these dead floors, win-
　　dows, rails—you call the church?
Why this is not the church at all—the Church is
　　living, ever living Souls.")

And you, America,
Cast you the real reckoning for your present?
The lights and shadows of your future—good or evil?
To girlhood, boyhood look—the Teacher and the
　　School.

## THOUGHTS

OF Public Opinion;
    Of a calm and cool fiat, sooner or later, (How
      impassive! How certain and final!)
Of the President with pale face, asking secretly to
    himself, *What will the people say at last?*
Of the frivolous Judge—Of the corrupt Congress-
    man, Governor, Mayor—Of such as these, stand-
    ing helpless and exposed;
Of the mumbling and screaming priest—(soon, soon
    deserted;)
Of the lessening, year by year, of venerableness, and
    of the dicta of officers, statutes, pulpits, schools;
Of the rising forever taller and stronger and broader,
    of the intuitions of men and women, and of self-
    esteem, and of personality;
—Of the New World—Of the Democracies, resplen-
    dent, en-masse;
Of the conformity of politics, armies, navies, to them
    and to me,
Of the shining sun by them—Of the inherent light,
    greater than the rest,
Of the envelopment of all by them, and of the effusion
    of all from them.


## WALT WHITMAN'S CAUTION

TO The States, or any one of them, or any city
    of The States, *Resist much, obey little;*
    Once unquestioning obedience, once fully
enslaved;
Once fully enslaved, no nation, state, city, of this
    earth, ever afterward resumes its liberty.

## ELECTION DAY, NOVEMBER, 1884

IF I should need to name, O Western World, your
    powerfulest scene and show,
    'Twould not be you, Niagara—nor you, ye
limitless prairies—nor your huge rifts of canyons,
    Colorado,
Nor you, Yosemite—nor Yellowstone, with all its
    spasmic geyserloops ascending to the skies, ap-
    pearing and disappearing,
Nor Oregon's white cones—nor Huron's belt of
    mighty lakes—nor Mississippi's stream:
—This seething hemisphere's humanity, as now, I'd
    name—*the still small voice* vibrating—America's
    choosing day,
(The heart of it not in the chosen—the act itself the
    main, the quadriennial choosing,)
The stretch of North and South arous'd—sea-board
    and inland—Texas to Maine—the Prairie States—
    Vermont, Virginia, California,
The final ballot-shower from East to West—the
    paradox and conflict,
The countless snow-flakes falling—(a swordless con-
    flict,
Yet more than all Rome's wars of old, or modern
    Napoleon's:) the peaceful choice of all,
Or good or ill humanity—welcoming the darker odds,
    the dross:
—Foams and ferments the wine? it serves to purify—
    while the heart pants, life glows:
These stormy gusts and winds waft precious ships,
Swell'd Washington's, Jefferson's, Lincoln's sails.

## WITH ALL THY GIFTS

WITH all thy gifts, America,
  (Standing secure, rapidly tending, overlook-
    ing the world,)
Power, wealth, extent, vouchsafed to thee—With
  these, and like of these, vouchsafed to thee,
What if one gift thou lackest? (the ultimate human
  problem never solving;)
The gift of Perfect Women fit for thee—What of that
  gift of gifts thou lackest?
The towering Feminine of thee? the beauty, health,
  completion, fit for thee?
The Mothers fit for thee?

## SAYS

1

I SAY whatever tastes sweet to the most perfect
  person, that is finally right.

2

I say nourish a great intellect, a great brain;
If I have said anything to the contrary, I hereby re-
  tract it.

3

I say man shall not hold property in man;
I say the least developed person on earth is just as
  important and sacred to himself or herself, as the
  most developed person is to himself or herself.

4

I say where liberty draws not the blood out of slavery,
  there slavery draws the blood out of liberty,
I say the word of the good old cause in These States,
  and resound it hence over the world.

### 5

I say the human shape or face is so great, it must
   never be made ridiculous;
I say for ornaments nothing outre can be allowed,
And that anything is most beautiful without orna-
   ment,
And that exaggerations will be sternly revenged in
   your own physiology, and in other persons' physi-
   ology also;
And I say that clean-shaped children can be jetted
   and conceived only where natural forms prevail
   in public, and the human face and form are never
   caricatured;
And I say that genius need never more be turned to
   romances,
(For facts properly told, how mean appear all ro-
   mances.)

### 6

I say the word of lands fearing nothing—I will have
   no other land;
I say discuss all and expose all—I am for every topic
   openly;
I say there can be no salvation for These States with-
   out innovators—without free tongues, and ears
   willing to hear the tongues;
And I announce as a glory of These States, that they
   respectfully listen to propositions, reforms, fresh
   views and doctrines, from successions of men and
   women,
Each age with its own growth.

## BEHAVIOR

BEHAVIOR—fresh, native, copious, each one
for himself or herself,
    Nature and the Soul expressed—America and
freedom expressed—In it the finest art,
In it pride, cleanliness, sympathy, to have their
chance,
In it physique, intellect, faith—in it just as much as
to manage an army or a city, or to write a book—
perhaps more,
The youth, the laboring person, the poor person,
rivalling all the rest—perhaps outdoing the rest,
The effects of the universe no greater than its;
For there is nothing in the whole universe that can
be more effective than a man's or woman's daily
behavior can be,
In any position, in any one of These States.


## THOUGHTS

### I

OF these years I sing,
    How they pass and have pass'd, through con-
vuls'd pains as through parturitions;
How America illustrates birth, muscular youth, the
promise, the sure fulfillment, the Absolute Suc-
cess, despite of people—Illustrates evil as well as
good;
How many hold despairingly yet to the models de-
parted, caste, myths, obedience, compulsion, and
to infidelity;
How few see the arrived models, the Athletes, the
Western States—or see freedom or spirituality—
or hold any faith in results,

(But I see the Athletes—and I see the results of the
war glorious and inevitable—and they again lead-
ing to other results;)
How the great cities appear—How the Democratic
masses, turbulent, wilful, as I love them;
How the whirl, the contest, the wrestle of evil with
good, the sounding and resounding, keep on and
on;
How society waits unform'd, and is for awhile be-
tween things ended and things begun;
How America is the continent of glories, and of the
triumph of freedom, and of the Democracies, and
of the fruits of society, and of all that is begun;
And how The States are complete in themselves—
And how all triumphs and glories are complete
in themselves, to lead onward,
And how these of mine, and of The States, will in
their turn be convuls'd, and serve other parturi-
tions and transitions,
And how all people, sights, combinations, the Dem-
ocratic masses, too, serve—and how every fact,
and war itself, with all its horrors, serves,
And how now, or at any time, each serves the ex-
quisite transition of death.

2

Of seeds dropping into the ground—of birth,
Of the steady concentration of America, inland, up-
ward, to impregnable and swarming places,
Of what Indiana, Kentucky, Ohio and the rest, are
to be,
Of what a few years will show there in Nebraska,
Colorado, Nevada, and the rest;
(Or afar, mounting the Northern Pacific to Sitka or
Alaska;)

72

Of what the feuillage of America is the preparation
for—and of what all sights, North, South, East
and West, are;
Of This Union, soak'd, welded in blood—of the
solemn price paid—of the unnamed lost, ever
present in my mind;
—Of the temporary use of materials, for identity's
sake,
Of the present, passing, departing—of the growth of
completer men than any yet,
Of myself, soon, perhaps, closing up my songs by
these shores,
Of California, of Oregon—and of me journeying to
live and sing there;
Of the Western Sea—of the spread inland between it
and the spinal river,
Of the great pastoral area, athletic and feminine,
Of all sloping down there where the fresh free giver,
the mother, the Mississippi flows,
Of future women there—of happiness in those high
plateaus, ranging three thousand miles, warm and
cold;
Of mighty inland cities yet unsurvey'd and un-
suspected, (as I am also, and as it must be;)
Of the new and good names—of the modern develop-
ments—of inalienable homesteads;
Of a free and original life there—of simple diet and
clean and sweet blood;
Of litheness, majestic faces, clear eyes, and perfect
physique there;
Of immense spiritual results, future years, far west,
each side of the Anahuacs;
Of these leaves, well understood there, (being made
for that area;)
Of the native scorn of grossness and gain there;
(O it lurks in me night and day—What is gain, after
all, to savageness and freedom?)

73

## LONG, TOO LONG, O LAND

LONG, too long, O land,
　　Traveling roads all even and peaceful, you
　　　learn'd from joys and prosperity only;
But now, ah now, to learn from crises of anguish—
　　advancing, grappling with direst fate, and re-
　　coiling not;
And now to conceive, and show to the world, what
　　your children en-masse really are;
(For who except myself has yet conceiv'd what your
　　children en-masse really are?)


## TO THEE, OLD CAUSE!

TO thee, old Cause!
　　Thou peerless, passionate, good cause!
　　Thou stern, remorseless, sweet Idea!
Deathless throughout the ages, races, lands!
After a strange, sad war—great war for thee,
(I think all war through time was really fought, and
　　ever will be really fought, for thee;)
These chants for thee—the eternal march of thee.

Thou orb of many orbs!
Thou seething principle! Thou well-kept, latent
　　germ! Thou centre!
Around the idea of thee the strange sad war revolving,
With all its angry and vehement play of causes,
(With yet unknown results to come, for thrice a
　　thousand years,)
These recitatives for thee—my Book and the War
　　are one,
Merged in its spirit I and mine—as the contest
　　hinged on thee,　　　　　　　　　　・
As a wheel on its axis turns, this Book, unwitting to
　　itself,
Around the Idea of thee.

## SONG OF THE BANNER AT DAY-BREAK

POET

O A NEW song, a free song,
   Flapping, flapping, flapping, flapping, by
   sounds, by voices clearer,
By the wind's voice and that of the drum,
By the banner's voice, and child's voice, and sea's
   voice, and father's voice,
Low on the ground and high in the air,
On the ground where father and child stand,
In the upward air where their eyes turn,
Where the banner at day-break is flapping.

Words! book-words! what are you?
Words no more, for hearken and see,
My song is there in the open air—and I must sing,
With the banner and pennant a-flapping.

I'll weave the chord and twine in,
Man's desire and babe's desire—I'll twine them in,
   I'll put in life;
I'll put the bayonet's flashing point—I'll let bullets
   and slugs whizz;
(As one carrying a symbol and menace, far into the
   future,
Crying with trumpet voice, *Arouse and beware! Be-
   ware and arouse!*)
I'll pour the verse with streams of blood, full of
   volition, full of joy;
Then loosen, launch forth, to go and compete,
With the banner and pennant a-flapping.

PENNANT

Come up here, bard, bard;
Come up here, soul, soul;
Come up here, dear little child,
To fly in the clouds and winds with me, and play with
   the measureless light.

75

### CHILD

Father, what is that in the sky beckoning to me with
  long finger?
And what does it say to me all the while?

### FATHER

Nothing, my babe, you see in the sky;
And nothing at all to you it says.  But look you, my
  babe,
Look at these dazzling things in the houses, and see
  you the money-shops opening;
And see you the vehicles preparing to crawl along
  the streets with goods:
These! ah, these! how valued and toil'd for, these!
How envied by all the earth!

### POET

Fresh and rosy red, the sun is mounting high;
On floats the sea in distant blue, careering through
  its channels;
On floats the wind over the breast of the sea, setting
  in toward land;
The great steady wind from west and west-by-south,
Floating so buoyant, with milk-white foam on the
  waters.

But I am not the sea, nor the red sun;
I am not the wind, with girlish laughter;
Not the immense wind which strengthens—not the
  wind which lashes;
Not the spirit that ever lashes its own body to terror
  and death;
But I am that which unseen comes and sings, sings,
  sings,
Which babbles in brooks and scoots in showers on the
  land,

Which the birds know in the woods, mornings and
    evenings,
And the shore-sands know, and the hissing wave, and
    that banner and pennant,
Aloft there flapping and flapping.

### CHILD

O father, it is alive—it is full of people—it has chil-
    dren!
O now it seems to me it is talking to its children!
I hear it—it talks to me—O it is wonderful!
O it stretches—it spreads and runs so fast! O my
    father,
It is so broad, it covers the whole sky!

### FATHER

Cease, cease, my foolish babe,
What you are saying is sorrowful to me—much it
    displeases me;
Behold with the rest, again I say—behold not ban-
    ners and pennants aloft;
But the well-prepared pavements behold—and mark
    the solid wall'd houses.

### BANNER AND PENNANT

Speak to the child, O bard, out of Manhattan;
(The war is over—yet never over . . . . out of it,
    we are born to real life and identity;)
Speak to our children all, or north or south of Man-
    hattan,
Where our factory-engines hum, where our miners
    delve the ground,
Where our hoarse Niagara rumbles, where our
    prairie-plows are plowing;
Speak, O bard! point this day, leaving all the rest, to
    us over all—and yet we know not why;

77

For what are we, mere strips of cloth, profiting
    nothing,
Only flapping in the wind?


### POET

I hear and see not strips of cloth alone;
I hear again the tramp of armies, I hear the chal-
    lenging sentry;
I hear the jubilant shouts of millions of men—I hear
    LIBERTY!
I hear the drums beat, and the trumpets yet blow-
    ing;
I myself move abroad, swift-rising, flying then;
I use the wings of the land-bird, and use the wings of
    the sea-bird, and look down as from a height;
I do not deny the precious results of peace—I see
    populous cities, with wealth incalculable;
I see numberless farms—I see the farmers working in
    their fields or barns;
I see mechanics working—I see buildings everywhere
    founded, going up, or finish'd;
I see trains of cars swiftly speeding along railroad
    tracks, drawn by the locomotives;
I see the stores, depots, of Boston, Baltimore,
    Charleston, New Orleans;
I see far in the west the immense area of grain—I
    dwell awhile, hovering;
I pass to the lumber forests of the north, and again
    to the southern plantation, and again to Cali-
    fornia;
Sweeping the whole, I see the countless profit, the
    busy gatherings, earned wages;
See the identity formed out of thirty-eight spacious
    and haughty States (and many more to come;)
See forts on the shores of harbors—see ships sailing
    in and out;

Then over all, (aye! aye!) my little and lengthen'd
  pennant, shaped like a sword,
Runs swiftly up, indicating war and defiance—And
  now the halyards have rais'd it,
Side of my banner broad and blue—side of my starry
  banner,
Discarding peace over all the sea and land.

## BANNER AND PENNANT

Yet louder, higher, stronger, bard! yet farther, wider
  cleave!
No longer let our children deem us riches and peace
  alone;
We may be terror and carnage, and are so now;
Not now are we any one of these spacious and
  haughty States, (nor any five, nor ten;)
Nor market nor depot are we, nor money-bank in the
  city;
But these, and all, and the brown and spreading
  land, and the mines below, are ours;
And the shores of the sea are ours, and the rivers,
  great and small;
And the fields they moisten are ours, and the crops
  and the fruits are ours;
Bays and channels, and ships sailing in and out, are
  ours—and we over all,
Over the area spread below, the three or four millions
  of square miles—the capitals,
The forty millions of people—O bard! in life and
  death supreme,
We, even we, henceforth flaunt out masterful, high
  up above,
Not for the present alone, for a thousand years,
  chanting through you,
This song to the soul of one poor little child.

### CHILD

O my father, I like not the houses;
They will never to me be anything—nor do I like
    money;
But to mount up there I would like, O father dear—
    that banner I like;
That pennant I would be, and must be.

### FATHER

Child of mine, you fill me with anguish;
To be that pennant would be too fearful;
Little you know what it is this day, and after this
    day, forever;
It is to gain nothing, but risk and defy everything;
Forward to stand in front of wars—and O, such
    wars! what have you to do with them?
With passions of demons, slaughter, premature
    death?

### POET

Demons and death then I sing;
Put in all, aye all, will I—sword-shaped pennant
    for war, and banner so broad and blue,
And a pleasure new and extatic, and the prattled
    yearning of children,
Blent with the sounds of the peaceful land, and the
    liquid wash of the sea;
And the black ships, fighting on the sea, enveloped
    in smoke;
And the icy cool of the far, far north, with rustling
    cedars and pines;
And the whirr of drums, and the sound of soldiers
    marching, and the hot sun shining south;
And the beech-waves combing over the beach on my
    eastern shore, and my western shore the same;
And all between those shores, and my ever running
    Mississippi, with bends and chutes;

And my Illinois fields, and my Kansas fields, and my
fields of Missouri;
The CONTINENT—devoting the whole identity, with-
out reserving an atom,
Pour in! whelm that which asks, which sings, with
all, and the yield of all.

## BANNER AND PENNANT

Aye all! for ever, for all!
From sea to sea, north and south, east and west,
(The war is completed, the price is paid, the title is
settled beyond recall;)
Fusing and holding, claiming, devouring the whole;
No more with tender lip, nor musical labial sound,
But, out of the night emerging for good, our voice
persuasive no more,
Croaking like crows here in the wind.

## POET

### (*Finale*)

My limbs, my veins dilate;
The blood of the world has fill'd me full—my theme
is clear at last:
—Banner so broad, advancing out of the night, I
sing you haughty and resolute;
I burst through where I waited long, too long,
deafen'd and blinded;
My sight, my hearing and tongue, are come to me,
(a little child taught me;)
I hear from above, O pennant of war, your ironical
call and demand;
Insensate! insensate! (yet I at any rate chant you,)
O banner!
Not houses of peace indeed are you, nor any nor all
their prosperity, (if need be, you shall again have
every one of those houses to destroy them;

6                          81

You thought not to destroy those valuable houses,
    standing fast, full of comfort, built with money;
May they stand fast, then? Not an hour, except
    you, above them and all, stand fast;)
—O banner! not money so precious are you, not
    farm produce you, nor the material good nutri-
    ment,
Nor excellent stores, nor landed on wharves from the
    ships;
Not the superb ships, with sail-power or steam-
    power, fetching and carrying cargoes,
Nor machinery, vehicles, trade, nor revenues,—
    But you, as henceforth I see you,
Running up out of the night, bringing your cluster
    of stars, (ever-enlarging stars;)
Divider of day-break you, cutting the air, touch'd by
    the sun, measuring the sky,
(Passionately seen and yearn'd for by one poor little
    child,
While others remain busy, or smartly talking, for-
    ever teaching thrift, thrift;)
O you up there! O pennant! where you undulate like
    a snake, hissing so curious,
Out of reach—an idea only—yet furiously fought for,
    risking bloody death—loved by me!
So loved! O you banner leading the day, with stars
    brought from the night!
Valueless, object of eyes, over all and demanding all
    —(absolute owner of ALL)—O banner and pen-
    nant!
I too leave the rest—great as it is, it is nothing—
    houses, machines are nothing—I see them not;
I see but you, O warlike pennant! O banner so broad,
    with stripes, I sing you only,
Flapping up there in the wind.

## RISE, O DAYS, FROM YOUR FATHOMLESS DEEPS

I

RISE, O days, from your fathomless deeps, till
    you loftier, fiercer sweep!
    Long for my soul, hungering gymnastic, I
devour'd what the earth gave me;
Long I roam'd the woods of the north—long I
    watch'd Niagara pouring;
I travel'd the prairies over, and slept on their breast
    —I cross'd the Nevadas, I cross'd the plateaus;
I ascended the towering rocks along the Pacific, I
    sail'd out to sea;
I sail'd through the storm, I was refresh'd by the
    storm;
I watch'd with joy the threatening maws of the
    waves;
I mark'd the white combs where they career'd so
    high, curling over;
I heard the wind piping, I saw the black clouds;
Saw from below what arose and mounted, (O superb!
    O wild as my heart, and powerful!)
Heard the continuous thunder, as it bellow'd after
    the lightning;
Noted the slender and jagged threads of lightning,
    as sudden and fast amid the din they chased each
    other across the sky;
—These, and such as these, I, elate, saw—saw with
    wonder, yet pensive and masterful;
All the menacing might of the globe uprisen around
    me;
Yet there with my soul I fed—I fed content, super-
    cilious.

2

'Twas well, O soul! 'twas a good preparation you
gave me!

Now we advance our latent and ampler hunger to
fill;

Now we go forth to receive what the earth and the
sea never gave us;

Not through the mighty woods we go, but through
the mightier cities;

Something for us is pouring now, more than Niagara
pouring;

Torrents of men, (sources and rills of the Northwest,
are you indeed inexhaustible?)

What, to pavements and homesteads here—what
were those storms of the mountains and sea?

What, to passions I witness around me to-day?  Was
the sea risen?

Was the wind piping the pipe of death under the
black clouds?

Lo! from deeps more unfathomable, something more
deadly and savage;

Manhattan, rising, advancing with menacing front—
Cincinnati, Chicago, unchain'd;

—What was that swell I saw on the ocean? behold
what comes here!

How it climbs with daring feet and hands! how it
dashes!

How the true thunder bellows after the lightning!
how bright the flashes of lightning!

How DEMOCRACY, with desperate vengeful port
strides on, shown through the dark by those flashes
of lightning!

(Yet a mournful wail and low sob I fancied I heard
through the dark,

In a lull of the deafening confusion.)

84

3

Thunder on! stride on, Democracy! strike with vengeful stroke!

And do you rise higher than ever yet, O days, O cities!

Crash heavier, heavier yet, O storms! you have done me good;

My soul, prepared in the mountains, absorbs your immortal strong nutriment;

—Long had I walk'd my cities, my country roads, through farms, only half-satisfied;

One doubt, nauseous, undulating like a snake, crawl'd on the ground before me,

Continually preceding my steps, turning upon me oft, ironically hissing low;

—The cities I loved so well, I abandon'd and left— I sped to the certainties suitable to me;

Hungering, hungering, hungering, for primal energies, and Nature's dauntlessness,

I refresh'd myself with it only, I could relish it only;

I waited the bursting forth of the pent fire—on the water and air I waited long;

—But now I no longer wait—I am fully satisfied—I am glutted;

I have witness'd the true lightning—I have witness'd my cities electric;

I have lived to behold man burst forth, and warlike America rise;

Hence I will seek no more the food of the northern solitary wilds,

No more on the mountains roam, or sail the stormy sea.

## A CAROL OF HARVEST, FOR 1867

### 1

A SONG of the good green grass!
A song no more of the city streets;
A song of farms—a song of the soil of fields.

A song with the smell of sun-dried hay, where the
nimble pitchers handle the pitch-fork;
A song tasting of new wheat, and of fresh-husk'd
maize.

### 2

For the lands, and for these passionate days, and for
myself,
Now I awhile return to thee, O soil of Autumn fields,
Reclining on thy breast, giving myself to thee,
Answering the pulses of thy sane and equable heart,
Tuning a verse for thee.

O Earth, that hast no voice, confide to me a voice!
O harvest of my lands! O boundless summer growths!
O lavish, brown, parturient earth! O infinite, teeming
womb!
A verse to seek, to see, to narrate thee.

### 3

Ever upon this stage,
Is acted God's calm, annual drama,
Gorgeous processions, songs of birds,
Sunrise, that fullest feeds and freshens most the soul,
The heaving sea, the waves upon the shore, the musi-
cal, strong waves,
The woods, the stalwart trees, the slender, tapering
trees,

The flowers, the grass, the lilliput, countless armies
   of the grass,
The heat, the showers, the measureless pasturages,
The scenery of the snows, the winds' free orchestra,
The stretching, light-hung roof of clouds—the clear
   cerulean, and the bulging, silvery fringes,
The high dilating stars, the placid, beckoning stars,
The moving flocks and herds, the plains and emerald
   meadows,
The shows of all the varied lands, and all the growths
   and products.


4

Fecund America!  To-day,
Thou art all over set in births and joys!
Thou groan'st with riches! thy wealth clothes thee
   as with a swathing garment!
Thou laughest loud with ache of great possessions!
A myriad-twining life, like interlacing vines, binds
   all thy vast demesne!
As some huge ship, freighted to water's edge, thou
   ridest into port!
As rain falls from the heaven, and vapors rise from
   earth, so have the precious values fallen upon thee,
   and risen out of thee!
Thou envy of the globe! thou miracle!
Thou, bathed, choked, swimming in plenty!
Thou lucky Mistress of the tranquil barns!
Thou Prairie Dame that sittest in the middle, and
   lookest out upon thy world, and lookest East, and
   lookest West!
Dispensatress, that by a word givest a thousand
   miles—that giv'st a million farms, and missest
   nothing!
Thou All-Acceptress—thou Hospitable—(thou only
   art hospitable, as God is hospitable.)

5

When late I sang, sad was my voice;
Sad were the shows around me, with deafening noises
of hatred, and smoke of conflict;
In the midst of the armies, the Heroes, I stood,
Or pass'd with slow step through the wounded and
dying.

But now I sing not War,
Nor the measur'd march of soldiers, nor the tents of
camps,
Nor the regiments hastily coming up, deploying in
line of battle.

No more the dead and wounded;
No more the sad, unnatural shows of War.
Ask'd room those flush'd immortal ranks? the first
forth-stepping armies?
Ask room, alas, the ghastly ranks—the armies dread
that follow'd.

6

(Pass—pass, ye proud brigades!
So handsome, dress'd in blue—with your tramping,
sinewy legs;
With your shoulders young and strong—with your
knapsacks and your muskets;
—How elate I stood and watch'd you, where, start-
ing off, you march'd!

Pass;—then rattle, drums, again!
Scream, you steamers on the river, out of whistles
loud and shrill, your salutes!
For an army heaves in sight—O another gathering
army!
Swarming, trailing on the rear—O you dread, ac-
cruing army!

O you regiments so piteous, with your mortal diar-
    rhœa! with your fever!
O my land's maimed darlings! with the plenteous
    bloody bandage and the crutch!
Lo! your pallid army follow'd!)

### 7

But on these days of brightness,
On the far-stretching beauteous landscape, the roads
    and lanes, the high-piled farm-wagons, and the
    fruits and barns,
Shall the dead intrude?

Ah, the dead to me mar not—they fit well in Nature;
They fit very well in the landscape, under the trees
    and grass,
And along the edge of the sky, in the horizon's far
    margin.

Nor do I forget you, departed;
Nor in winter or summer, my lost ones;
But most, in the open air, as now, when my soul is
    rapt and at peace—like pleasing phantoms,
Your dear memories, rising, glide silently by me.

### 8

I saw the day, the return of the Heroes;
(Yet the Heroes never surpass'd, shall never return;
Them, that day, I saw not.)

I saw the interminable Corps—I saw the processions
    of armies,
I saw them approaching, defiling by, with divisions,
Streaming northward, their work done, camping
    awhile in clusters of mighty camps.

No holiday soldiers—youthful, yet veterans;
Worn, swart, handsome, strong, of the stock of
    homestead and workshop,

Harden'd of many a long campaign and sweaty
     march,
Inured on many a hard-fought, bloody field.


9

A pause—the armies wait;
A million flush'd, embattled conquerors wait;
The world, too, waits—then, soft as breaking night,
     and sure as dawn,
They melt—they disappear.

Exult, indeed, O lands! victorious lands!
Not there your victory, on those red, shuddering
     fields;
But here and hence your victory.

Melt, melt away, ye armies! disperse, ye blue-clad
     soldiers!
Resolve ye back again—give up, for good, your
     deadly arms;
Other the arms, the fields henceforth for you, or
     South or North, or East or West,
With saner wars—sweet wars—life-giving wars.


10

Loud, O my throat, and clear, O soul!
The season of thanks, and the voice of full-yielding;
The chant of joy and power for boundless fertility.

All till'd and untill'd fields expand before me;
I see the true arenas of my race—or first, or last,
Man's innocent and strong arenas.

I see the Heroes at other toils;
I see, well-wielded in their hands, the better weapons.

## 11

I see where America, Mother of All,
Well-pleased, with full-spanning eye, gazes forth,
     dwells long,
And counts the varied gathering of the products.

Busy the far, the sunlit panorama;
Prairie, orchard, and yellow grain of the North,
Cotton and rice of the South, and Louisianian cane;
Open, unseeded fallows, rich fields of clover and
     timothy,
Kine and horses feeding, and droves of sheep and
     swine,
And many a stately river flowing, and many a jocund
     brook,
And healthy uplands with their herby-perfumed
     breezes,
And the good green grass—that delicate miracle, the
     ever-recurring grass.

## 12

Toil on, Heroes! harvest the products!
Not alone on those warlike fields, the Mother of All,
With dilated form and lambent eyes, watch'd you.

Toil on, Heroes! toil well!   Handle the weapons well!
The Mother of All—yet here, as ever, she watches
     you.

Well-pleased, America, thou beholdest,
Over the fields of the West, those crawling monsters,
The human-divine inventions, the labor-saving im-
     plements;
Beholdest, moving in every direction, imbued as
     with life, the revolving hay-rakes,
The steam-power reaping-machines, and the horse-
     power machines,

The engines, thrashers of grain, and cleaners of grain,
  well separating the straw—the nimble work of the
  patent pitch-fork;
Beholdest the newer saw-mill, the southern cotton-
  gin, and the rice-cleanser.

Beneath thy look, O Maternal,
With these, and else, and with their own strong
  hands, the Heroes harvest.

All gather, and all harvest;
(Yet but for thee, O Powerful! not a scythe might
  swing, as now, in security;
Not a maize-stalk dangle, as now, its silken tassels in
  peace.)

13

Under Thee only they harvest—even but a wisp of
  hay, under thy great face, only;
Harvest the wheat of Ohio, Illinois, Wisconsin—
  every barbed spear, under thee;
Harvest the maize of Missouri, Kentucky, Tennessee
  —each ear in its light-green sheath,
Gather the hay to its myriad mows, in the odorous,
  tranquil barns,
Oats to their bins—the white potato, the buckwheat
  of Michigan, to theirs;
Gather the cotton in Mississippi or Alabama—dig
  and hoard the golden, the sweet potato of Georgia
  and the Carolinas,
Clip the wool of California or Pennsylvania,
Cut the flax in the Middle States, or hemp, or to-
  bacco in the Borders,
Pick the pea and the bean, or pull apples from the
  trees, or bunches of grapes from the vines,
Or aught that ripens in all These States, or North or
  South,
Under the beaming sun, and under Thee.

## BATHED IN WAR'S PERFUME

BATHED in war's perfume—delicate flag!
  (Should the days needing armies, needing
    fleets, come again,)
O to hear you call the sailors and the soldiers! flag
  like a beautiful woman!
O to hear the tramp, tramp, of a million answering
  men! O the ships they arm with joy!
O to see you leap and beckon from the tall masts of
  ships!
O to see you peering down on the sailors on the decks!
Flag like the eyes of women.


## TURN, O LIBERTAD

TURN, O Libertad, for the war is over,
  (From it and all henceforth expanding, doubt-
    ing no more, resolute, sweeping the world,)
Turn from lands retrospective, recording proofs of
  the past;
From the singers that sing the trailing glories of the
  past;
From the chants of the feudal world—the triumphs of
  kings, slavery, caste;
Turn to the world, the triumphs reserv'd and to
  come—give up that backward world;
Leave to the singers of hitherto—give them the
  trailing past;
But what remains, remains for singers for you—wars
  to come are for you;
(Lo! how the wars of the past have duly inured to
  you—and the wars of the present also inure:)
—Then turn, and be not alarm'd, O Libertad—turn
  your undying face,
To where the future, greater than all the past,
Is swiftly, surely preparing for you.

93

## O SUN OF REAL PEACE

O SUN of real peace! O hastening light!
O free and extatic! O what I here, preparing,
    warble for!
O the sun of the world will ascend, dazzling, and take
    his height—and you too, O my Ideal, will surely
    ascend!
O so amazing and broad—up there resplendent,
    darting and burning!
O vision prophetic, stagger'd with weight of light!
    with pouring glories!
O lips of my soul, already becoming powerless!
O ample and grand Presidentiads!  Now the war, the
    war is over!
New history! new heroes! I project you!
Visions of poets! only you really last! sweep on!
    sweep on!
O heights too swift and dizzy yet!
O purged and luminous! you threaten me more than
    I can stand!
(I must not venture—the ground under my feet
    menaces me—it will not support me:
O future too immense,)—O present, I return, while
    yet I may, to you.

## AS I SAT ALONE BY BLUE ONTARIO'S SHORE

### 1

A S I sat alone, by blue Ontario's shore,
  As I mused of these mighty days, and of peace
    return'd, and the dead that return no more,
A Phantom, gigantic, superb, with stern visage,
  accosted me;
*Chant me the poem*, it said, *that comes from the soul of
  America—chant me the carol of victory;*
*And strike up the marches of Libertad—marches more
  powerful yet;*
*And sing me before you go, the song of the throes of
  Democracy.*

(Democracy—the destin'd conqueror—yet treacher-
  ous lip-smiles everywhere,
And Death and infidelity at every step.)

### 2

A Nation announcing itself,
I myself make the only growth by which I can be
  appreciated,
I reject none, accept all, then reproduce all in my own
  forms.

A breed whose proof is in time and deeds;
What we are, we are—nativity is answer enough to
  objections;
We wield ourselves as a weapon is wielded,
We are powerful and tremendous in ourselves,
We are executive in ourselves—We are sufficient in
  the variety of ourselves,
We are the most beautiful to ourselves, and in our-
  selves;

95

We stand self-pois'd in the middle, branching thence
    over the world;
From Missouri, Nebraska, or Kansas, laughing
    attacks to scorn.

Nothing is sinful to us outside of ourselves,
Whatever appears, whatever does not appear, we are
    beautiful or sinful in ourselves only.

(O mother!  O sisters dear!
If we are lost, no victor else has destroy'd us;
It is by ourselves we go down to eternal night.)

3

Have you thought there could be but a single
    Supreme?
There can be any number of Supremes—One does
    not countervail another, any more than one eye-
    sight countervails another, or one life countervails
    another.

All is eligible to all,
All is for individuals—All is for you,
No condition is prohibited—not God's, or any.

All comes by the body—only health puts you rapport
    with the universe.

Produce great persons, the rest follows.

4

America isolated I sing;
I say that works made here in the spirit of other
    lands, are so much poison in The States.

(How dare such insects as we see assume to write
    poems for America?
For our victorious armies, and the offspring following
    the armies?)

Piety and conformity to them that like!
Peace, obesity, allegiance, to them that like!
I am he who tauntingly compels men, women, na-
tions,
Crying, Leap from your seats, and contend for your
lives!

I am he who walks the States with a barb'd tongue,
questioning every one I meet;
Who are you, that wanted only to be told what you
knew before?
Who are you, that wanted only a book to join you in
your nonsense?

(With pangs and cries, as thine own, O bearer of
many children!
These clamors wild, to a race of pride I give.)

O lands! would you be freer than all that has ever
been before?
If you would be freer than all that has been before,
come listen to me.

Fear grace—Fear elegance, civilization, delicatesse,
Fear the mellow sweet, the sucking of honey-juice;
Beware the advancing mortal ripening of nature,
Beware what precedes the decay of the ruggedness of
states and men.

5

Ages, precedents, have long been accumulating un-
directed materials,
America brings builders, and brings its own styles.

The immortal poets of Asia and Europe have done
their work, and pass'd to other spheres,
A work remains, the work of surpassing all they have
done.

7

America, curious toward foreign characters, stands
  by its own at all hazards,
Stands removed, spacious, composite, sound—initi-
  ates the true use of precedents,
Does not repel them, or the past, or what they have
  produced under their forms,
Takes the lesson with calmness, perceives the corpse
  slowly borne from the house,
Perceives that it waits a little while in the door—
  that it was fittest for its days,
That its life has descended to the stalwart and well-
  shaped heir who approaches,
And that he shall be fittest for his days.

Any period, one nation must lead,
One land must be the promise and reliance of the
  future.

These States are the amplest poem,
Here is not merely a nation, but a teeming nation of
  nations,
Here the doings of men correspond with the broad-
  cast doings of the day and night,
Here is what moves in magnificent masses, careless of
  particulars,
Here are the roughs, beards, friendliness, combative-
  ness, the Soul loves,
Here the flowing trains—here the crowds, equality,
  diversity, the Soul loves.


6

Land of lands, and bards to corroborate!
Of them, standing among them, one lifts to the light
  his west-bred face,
To him the hereditary countenance bequeath'd, both
  mother's and father's,

98

His first parts substances, earth, water, animals, trees,
Built of the common stock, having room for far and
near,
Used to dispense with other lands, incarnating this
land,
Attracting it Body and Soul to himself, hanging on its
neck with incomparable love,
Plunging his seminal muscle into its merits and
demerits,
Making its cities, beginnings, events, diversities,
wars, vocal in him,
Making its rivers, lakes, bays, embouchure in him,
Mississippi with yearly freshets and changing chutes
—Columbia, Niagara, Hudson, spending them-
selves lovingly in him,
If the Atlantic coast stretch, or the Pacific coast
stretch, he stretching with them north or south,
Spanning between them, east and west, and touching
whatever is between them,
Growths growing from him to offset the growth of
pine, cedar, hemlock, live-oak, locust, chestnut,
hickory, cottonwood, orange, magnolia,
Tangles as tangled in him as any cane-brake or
swamp,
He likening sides and peaks of mountains, forests
coated with northern transparent ice,
Off him pasturage, sweet and natural as savanna, up-
land, prairie,
Through him flights, whirls, screams, answering
those of the fish-hawk, mocking-bird, night-heron,
and eagle;
His spirit surrounding his country's spirit, unclosed
to good and evil,
Surrounding the essences of real things, old times and
present times,
Surrounding just found shores, islands, tribes of red
aborigines,

Weather-beaten vessels, landings, settlements, em-
  bryo stature and muscle,
The haughty defiance of the Year 1—war, peace, the
  formation of the Constitution,
The separate States, the simple, elastic scheme, the
  immigrants,
The Union, always swarming with blatherers, and
  always sure and impregnable,
The unsurvey'd interior, log houses, clearings, wild
  animals, hunters, trappers;
Surrounding the multiform agriculture, mines, tem-
  perature, the gestation of new States,
Congress convening every Twelfth-month, the
  members duly coming up from the uttermost
  parts;
Surrounding the noble character of mechanics and
  farmers, especially the young men,
Responding their manners, speech, dress, friendships
  —the gait they have of persons who never knew
  how it felt to stand in the presence of superiors,
The freshness and candor of their physiognomy, the
  copiousness and decision of their phrenology,
The picturesque looseness of their carriage, their
  fierceness when wrong'd,
The fluency of their speech, their delight in music,
  their curiosity, good temper, and open-handedness
  —the whole composite make,
The prevailing ardor and enterprise, the large ama-
  tiveness,
The perfect equality of the female with the male, the
  fluid movement of the population,
The superior marine, free commerce, fisheries, whal-
  ing, gold-digging,
Wharf-hemm'd cities, railroad and steamboat lines,
  intersecting all points,
Factories, mercantile life, labor-saving machinery,
  the north-east, north-west, south-west,

Manhattan firemen, the Yankee swap, southern
plantation life,
Slavery—the murderous, treacherous conspiracy to
raise it upon the ruins of all the rest;
On and on to the grapple with it—Assassin! then
your life or ours be the stake—and respite no
more.

7

(Lo! high toward heaven, this day,
Libertad! from the conqueress' field return'd,
I mark the new aureola around your head;
No more of soft astral, but dazzling and fierce,
With war's flames, and the lambent lightnings play-
ing,
And your port immovable where you stand;
With still the inextinguishable glance, and the
clench'd and lifted fist,
And your foot on the neck of the menacing one, the
scorner, utterly crush'd beneath you;
The menacing, arrogant one, that strode and ad-
vanced with his senseless scorn, bearing the
murderous knife;
—Lo! the wide swelling one, the braggart, that would
yesterday do so much!
To-day a carrion dead and damn'd, the despised of all
the earth!
An offal rank, to the dunghill maggots spurn'd.)

8

Others take finish, but the Republic is ever con-
structive, and ever keeps vista;
Others adorn the past—but you, O days of the pre-
sent, I adorn you!
O days of the future, I believe in you! I isolate my-
self for your sake;

O America, because you build for mankind, I build
for you!
O well-beloved stone-cutters! I lead them who plan
with decision and science,
I lead the present with friendly hand toward the
future.

Bravas to all impulses sending sane children to the
next age!
But damn that which spends itself, with no thought
of the stain, pains, dismay, feebleness it is be-
queathing.

9

I listened to the Phantom by Ontario's shore,
I heard the voice arising, demanding bards;
By them, all native and grand—by them alone can
The States be fused into the compact organism of a
Nation.

To hold men together by paper and seal, or by com-
pulsion, is no account;
That only holds men together which aggregates all in
a living principle, as the hold of the limbs of the
body, or the fibres of plants.

Of all races and eras, These States, with veins full of
poetical stuff, most need poets, and are to have the
greatest, and use them the greatest;
Their Presidents shall not be their common referee
so much as their poets shall.

(Soul of love, and tongue of fire!
Eye to pierce the deepest deeps, and sweep the
world!
—Ah, mother! prolific and full in all besides—yet
how long barren, barren?)

10

Of These States, the poet is the equable man,
Not in him, but off from him, things are grotesque,
eccentric, fail of their full returns,
Nothing out of its place is good, nothing in its place
is bad,
He bestows on every object or quality its fit propor-
tion, neither more nor less,
He is the arbiter of the diverse, he is the key,
He is the equalizer of his age and land,
He supplies what wants supplying—he checks what
wants checking,
In peace, out of him speaks the spirit of peace, large,
rich, thrifty, building populous towns, encouraging
agriculture, arts, commerce, lighting the study of
man, the Soul, health, immortality, government;
In war, he is the best backer of the war—he fetches
artillery as good as the engineer's—he can make
every word he speaks draw blood;
The years straying toward infidelity, he withholds by
his steady faith,
He is no arguer, he is judgment—(Nature accepts
him absolutely;)
He judges not as the judge judges, but as the sun
falling round a helpless thing;
As he sees the farthest, he has the most faith,
His thoughts are the hymns of the praise of
things,
In the dispute on God and eternity he is silent,
He sees eternity less like a play with a prologue and
denouement,
He sees eternity in men and women—he does not see
men and women as dreams or dots.


For the great Idea, the idea of perfect and free
individuals,

For that idea the bard walks in advance, leader of
   leaders,
The attitude of him cheers up slaves and horrifies
   foreign despots.

Without extinction is Liberty! without retrograde is
   Equality!
They live in the feelings of young men, and the best
   women;
Not for nothing have the indomitable heads of the
   earth been always ready to fall for Liberty.


11

For the great Idea!
That, O my brethren—that is the mission of Poets.

Songs of stern defiance, ever ready,
Songs of the rapid arming, and the march,
The flag of peace quick-folded, and instead, the flag
   we know,
Warlike flag of the great Idea.

(Angry cloth I saw there leaping!
I stand again in leaden rain, your flapping folds
   saluting;
I sing you over all, flying, beckoning through the
   fight—O the hard-contested fight!
O the cannons ope their rosy-flashing muzzles! the
   hurtled balls scream!
The battle-front forms amid the smoke—the volleys
   pour incessant from the line;
Hark! the ringing word, *Charge!*—now the tussle,
   and the furious maddening yells;
Now the corpses tumble curl'd upon the ground,
Cold, cold in death, for precious life of you,
Angry cloth I saw there leaping.)

12

Are you he who would assume a place to teach, or be
a poet here in The States?
The place is august—the terms obdurate.

Who would assume to teach here, may well prepare
himself, body and mind,
He may well survey, ponder, arm, fortify, harden,
make lithe, himself,
He shall surely be question'd beforehand by me with
many and stern questions.

Who are you, indeed, who would talk or sing to
America?
Have you studied out the land, its idioms and
men?
Have you learn'd the physiology, phrenology, poli-
tics, geography, pride, freedom, friendship, of the
land? its substratums and objects?
Have you consider'd the organic compact of the first
day of the first year of Independence, sign'd by the
Commissioners, ratified by The States, and read by
Washington at the head of the army?
Have you possess'd yourself of the Federal Constitu-
tion?
Do you see who have left all feudal processes and
poems behind them, and assumed the poems and
processes of Democracy?
Are you faithful to things? do you teach as the land
and sea, the bodies of men, womanhood, amative-
ness, angers, teach?
Have you sped through fleeting customs, populari-
ties?
Can you hold your hand against all seductions, fol-
lies, whirls, fierce contentions? are you very strong?
are you really of the whole people?

Are you not of some coterie? some school or mere
religion?
Are you done with reviews and criticisms of life?
animating now to life itself?
Have you vivified yourself from the maternity of
These States?
Have you too the old, ever-fresh forbearance and
impartiality?
Do you hold the like love for those hardening to
maturity; for the last-born? little and big? and for
the errant?

What is this you bring my America?
Is it uniform with my country?
Is it not something that has been better told or done
before?
Have you not imported this, or the spirit of it, in
some ship?
Is it not a mere tale? a rhyme? a prettiness? is the
good old cause in it?
Has it not dangled long at the heels of the poets,
politicians, literats, of enemies' lands?
Does it not assume that what is notoriously gone is
still here?
Does it answer universal needs? will it improve
manners?
Does it sound, with trumpet-voice, the proud victory
of the Union, in that secession war?
Can your performance face the open fields and the
seaside?
Will it absorb into me as I absorb food, air—to
appear again in my strength, gait, face?
Have real employments contributed to it? original
makers—not mere amanuenses?
Does it meet modern discoveries, calibers, facts face
to face?

What does it mean to me? to American persons,
   progresses, cities? Chicago, Kanada, Arkansas?
   the planter, Yankee, Georgian, native, immigrant,
   sailors, squatters, old States, new States?
Does it encompass all The States, and the unexcep-
   tional rights of all the men and women of the
   earth? (the genital impulse of These States;)
Does it see behind the apparent custodians, the
   real custodians, standing, menacing, silent—the
   mechanics, Manhattanese, western men, southern-
   ers, significant alike in their apathy, and in the
   promptness of their love?
Does it see what finally befalls, and has always
   finally befallen, each temporizer, patcher, out-
   sider, partialist, alarmist, infidel, who has ever
   ask'd anything of America?
What mocking and scornful negligence?
The track strew'd with the dust of skeletons;
By the roadside others disdainfully toss'd.

13

Rhymes and rhymers pass away—poems distill'd
   from foreign poems pass away,
The swarms of reflectors and the polite pass, and
   leave ashes;
Admirers, importers, obedient persons, make but
   the soil of literature;
America justifies itself, give it time—no disguise can
   deceive it, or conceal from it—it is impassive
   enough,
Only toward the likes of itself will it advance to
   meet them,
If its poets appear, it will in due time advance to
   meet them—there is no fear of mistake,
(The proof of a poet shall be sternly deferr'd, till his
   country absorbs him as affectionately as he has
   absorb'd it.)

He masters whose spirit masters—he tastes sweetest
  who results sweetest in the long run;
The blood of the brawn beloved of time is uncon-
  straint;
In the need of poems, philosophy, politics, manners,
  engineering, an appropriate native grand-opera,
  shipcraft, any craft, he or she is greatest who con-
  tributes the greatest original practical example.


Already a nonchalant breed, silently emerging,
  appears on the streets,
People's lips salute only doers, lovers, satisfiers,
  positive knowers;
There will shortly be no more priests—I say their
  work is done,
Death is without emergencies here, but life is per-
  petual emergencies here,
Are your body, days, manners, superb? after death
  you shall be superb;
Justice, health, self-esteem, clear the way with
  irresistible power;
How dare you place anything before a man?


14

Fall behind me, States!
A man before all—myself, typical before all.


Give me the pay I have served for!
Give me to sing the song of the great Idea! take all
  the rest;
I have loved the earth, sun, animals—I have
  despised riches,
I have given alms to every one that ask'd, stood up
  for the stupid and crazy, devoted my income and
  labor to others,

I have hated tyrants, argued not concerning God,
  had patience and indulgence toward the people,
  taken off my hat to nothing known or unknown,
I have gone freely with powerful uneducated persons,
  and with the young, and with the mothers of
  families,
I have read these leaves to myself in the open air—I
  have tried them by trees, stars, rivers,
I have dismiss'd whatever insulted my own Soul or
  defiled my Body,
I have claim'd nothing to myself which I have not
  carefully claim'd for others on the same terms,
I have sped to the camps, and comrades found and
  accepted from every State;
(In war of you, as well as peace, my suit is good,
  America—sadly I boast;
Upon this breast has many a dying soldier lean'd,
  to breathe his last;
This arm, this hand, this voice, have nourish'd,
  rais'd, restored,
To life recalling many a prostrate form:)
—I am willing to wait to be understood by the
  growth of the taste of myself,
I reject none, I permit all.

(Say, O mother! have I not to your thought been
  faithful?
Have I not, through life, kept you and yours before
  me?)

15

I swear I begin to see the meaning of these things!
It is not the earth, it is not America, who is so
  great,
It is I who am great, or to be great—it is you up
  there, or any one;
It is to walk rapidly through civilizations, govern-
  ments, theories,

Through poems, pageants, shows, to form great in-
dividuals.

Underneath all, individuals!
I swear nothing is good to me now that ignores in-
dividuals,
The American compact is altogether with individuals,
The only government is that which makes minute of
individuals,
The whole theory of the universe is directed to one
single individual—namely, to You.

(Mother! with subtle sense severe—with the naked
sword in your hand,
I saw you at last refuse to treat but directly with
individuals.)

16

Underneath all, nativity,
I swear I will stand by my own nativity—pious or
impious, so be it;
I swear I am charm'd with nothing except nativity,
Men, women, cities, nations, are only beautiful from
nativity.

Underneath all is the need of the expression of love
for men and women,
I swear I have seen enough of mean and impotent
modes of expressing love for men and women,
After this day I take my own modes of expressing
love for men and women.

I swear I will have each quality of my race in my-
self,
Talk as you like, he only suits These States whose
manners favor the audacity and sublime turbulence
of The States.)

Underneath the lessons of things, spirits, Nature,
  governments, ownerships, I swear I perceive other
  lessons,
Underneath all, to me is myself—to you, yourself—
  (the same monotonous old song.)


17

O I see now, flashing, that this America is only you
  and me,
Its power, weapons, testimony, are you and me,
Its crimes, lies, thefts, defections, slavery, are you
  and me,
Its Congress is you and me—the officers, capitols,
  armies, ships, are you and me,
Its endless gestations of new States are you and
  me,
The war—that war so bloody and grim—the war I
  will henceforth forget—was you and me,
Natural and artificial are you and me,
Freedom, language, poems, employments, are you
  and me,
Past, present, future, are you and me.


18

I swear I dare not shirk any part of myself,
Not any part of America, good or bad,
Not the promulgation of Liberty—not to cheer up
  slaves and horrify foreign despots,
Not to build for that which builds for mankind,
Not to balance ranks, complexions, creeds, and the
  sexes,
Not to justify science, nor the march of equality,
Nor to feed the arrogant blood of the brawn beloved
  of time.

I swear I am for those that have never been master'd!
For men and women whose tempers have never been
    master'd,
For those whom laws, theories, conventions, can
    never master.

I swear I am for those who walk abreast with the
    whole earth!
Who inaugurate one, to inaugurate all.

I swear I will not be outfaced by irrational things!
I will penetrate what it is in them that is sarcastic
    upon me!
I will make cities and civilizations defer to me!
This is what I have learnt from America—it is the
    amount—and it I teach again.

(Democracy! while weapons were everywhere aim'd
    at your breast,
I saw you serenely give birth to immortal children—
    saw in dreams your dilating form;
Saw you with spreading mantle covering the world.)


19

I will confront these shows of the day and night!
I will know if I am to be less than they!
I will see if I am not as majestic as they!
I will see if I am not as subtle and real as they!
I will see if I am to be less generous than they!
I will see if I have no meaning, while the houses
    and ships have meaning!
I will see if the fishes and birds are to be enough for
    themselves, and I am not to be enough for myself.

20

I match my spirit against yours, you orbs, growths,
   mountains, brutes,
Copious as you are, I absorb you all in myself, and
   become the master myself.

America isolated, yet embodying all, what is it
   finally except myself?
These States—what are they except myself?

I know now why the earth is gross, tantalizing,
   wicked—it is for my sake,
I take you to be mine, you beautiful, terrible, rude
   forms.

(Mother! bend down, bend close to me your face!
I know not what these plots and wars, and defer-
   ments are for;
I know not fruition's success—but I know that
   through war and peace your work goes on, and
   must yet go on.)

21

.   .   .   .   Thus, by blue Ontario's shore,
While the winds fann'd me, and the waves came
   trooping toward me,
I thrill'd with the Power's pulsations—and the charm
   of my theme was upon me,
Till the tissues that held me, parted their ties upon
   me.

And I saw the free Souls of poets;
The loftiest bards of past ages strode before me,
Strange, large men, long unwaked, undisclosed, were
   disclosed to me.

8

22

O my rapt verse, my call—mock me not!
Not for the bards of the past—not to invoke them
    have I launch'd you forth,
Not to call even those lofty bards here by Ontario's
    shores,
Have I sung so capricious and loud, my savage song.

Bards for my own land, only, I invoke;
(For the war, the war is over—the field is clear'd,)
Till they strike up marches henceforth triumphant
    and onward,
To cheer, O mother, your boundless, expectant soul.

Bards grand as these days so grand!
Bards of the great Idea! Bards of the peaceful in-
    ventions! (for the war, the war is over!)
Yet Bards of the latent armies—a million soldiers
    waiting, ever-ready,
Bards towering like hills—(no more these dots,
    these pigmies, these little piping straws, these
    gnats, that fill the hour, to pass for poets;)
Bards with songs as from burning coals, or the
    lightning's fork'd stripes!
Ample Ohio's bards—bards for California! inland
    bards—bards of the war;
(As a wheel turns on its axle, so I find my chants
    turning finally on the war;)
Bards of pride! Bards tallying the ocean's roar, and
    the swooping eagle's scream!
You, by my charm, I invoke!

## AS I WALK THESE BROAD, MAJESTIC DAYS

AS I walk these broad, majestic days of peace,
(For the war, the struggle of blood finish'd,
wherein, O terrific Ideal!
Against vast odds, having gloriously won,
Now thou stridest on—yet perhaps in time toward
denser wars,
Perhaps to engage in time in still more dreadful
contests, dangers,
Longer campaigns and crises, labors beyond all
others;)
—As I walk solitary, unattended,
Around me I hear that eclat of the world—politics,
produce,
The announcements of recognized things—science,
The approved growth of cities, and the spread of in-
ventions.


I see the ships, (they will last a few years,)
The vast factories, with their foremen and work-
men,
And here the indorsement of all, and do not object
to it.


But I too announce solid things;
Science, ships, politics, cities, factories, are not
nothing—I watch them,
Like a grand procession, to music of distant bugles,
pouring, triumphantly moving—and grander heav-
ing in sight;
They stand for realities—all is as it should be.

Then my realities;
What else is so real as mine?
Libertad, and the divine average—Freedom to every
    slave on the face of the earth,
The rapt promises and luminé of seers—the spiritual
    world—these centuries-lasting songs,
And our visions, the visions of poets, the most solid
    announcements of any.

For we support all, fuse all,
After the rest is done and gone, we remain;
There is no final reliance but upon us;
Democracy rests finally upon us (I, my brethren,
    begin it,)
And our visions sweep through eternity.


WASHINGTON'S MONUMENT, FEBRUARY,
1885

AH, not this marble, dead and cold:
    Far from its base and shaft expanding—the
        round zones circling, comprehending,
Thou, Washington, art all the world's, the conti-
    nents' entire—not yours alone, America,
Europe's as well, in every part, castle of lord or
    laborer's cot,
Or frozen North, or sultry South—the African's—
    the Arab's in his tent,
Old Asia's there with venerable smile, seated amid
    her ruins;
(Greets the antique the hero new? 'tis but the same
    —the heir legitimate, continued ever,
The indomitable heart and arm—proofs of the
    never-broken line,
Courage, alertness, patience, faith, the same—e'en in
    defeat defeated not, the same:)

Wherever sails a ship, or house is built on land, or
    day or night,
Through teeming cities' streets, indoors or out, fac-
    tories or farms,
Now, or to come, or past—where patriot wills existed
    or exist,
Wherever Freedom, pois'd by Toleration, sway'd by
    Law,
Stands or is rising thy true monument.


## THE UNITED STATES TO OLD WORLD
## CRITICS

HERE first the duties of to-day, the lessons of
    the concrete,
      Wealth, order, travel, shelter, products,
plenty;
As of the building of some varied, vast, perpetual
    edifice,
Whence to arise inevitable in time, the towering
    roofs, the lamps,
The solid-planted spires tall shooting to the stars.

## BROTHER OF ALL, WITH GENEROUS HAND

### (G. P., BURIED FEBRUARY, 1870)

1

BROTHER of all, with generous hand,
  Of thee, pondering on thee, as o'er thy tomb,
    I and my Soul,
A thought to launch in memory of thee,
A burial verse for thee.

What may we chant, O thou within this tomb?
What tablets, pictures, hang for thee, O million-
  aire?
—The life thou lived'st we know not,
But that thou walk'dst thy years in barter, 'mid the
  haunts of brokers;
Nor heroism thine, nor war, nor glory.

Yet lingering, yearning, joining soul with thine,
If not thy past we chant, we chant the future,
Select, adorn the future.

2

Lo, Soul, the graves of heroes!
The pride of lands—the gratitudes of men,
The statues of the manifold famous dead, Old World
  and New,
The kings, inventors, generals, poets, (stretch wide
  thy vision, Soul,)
The excellent rulers of the races, great discoverers,
  sailors,
Marble and brass select from them, with pictures,
  scenes,
(The histories of the lands, the races, bodied there,
In what they've built for, graced and graved,
Monuments to their heroes.)

3

Silent, my Soul,
With drooping lids, as waiting, ponder'd,
Turning from all the samples, all the monuments of
heroes.


While through the interior vistas,
Noiseless uprose, phantasmic (as, by night, Auroras
of the North,)
Lambent tableaux, prophetic, bodiless scenes,
Spiritual projections.


In one, among the city streets, a laborer's home ap-
pear'd,
After his day's work done, cleanly, sweet-air'd, the
gaslight burning,
The carpet swept, and a fire in the cheerful stove.


In one, the sacred parturition scene,
A happy, painless mother birth'd a perfect child.


In one, at a bounteous morning meal,
Sat peaceful parents, with contented sons.


In one, by twos and threes, young people,
Hundreds concentering, walk'd the paths and streets
and roads,
Toward a tall-domed school.


In one a trio, beautiful,
Grandmother, loving daughter, loving daughter's
daughter, sat,
Chatting and sewing.

In one, along a suite of noble rooms,
'Mid plenteous books and journals, paintings on the
    walls, fine statuettes,
Were groups of friendly journeymen, mechanics,
    young and old,
Reading, conversing.

All, all the shows of laboring life,
City and country, women's, men's and children's,
Their wants provided for, hued in the sun, and tinged
    for once with joy,
Marriage, the street, the factory, farm, the house-
    room, lodging-room,
Labor and toil, the bath, gymnasium, play-ground,
    library, college,
The student, boy or girl, led forward to be taught;
The sick cared for, the shoeless shod—the orphan
    father'd and mother'd,
The hungry fed, the houseless housed;
(The intentions perfect and divine,
The workings, details, haply human.)

4

O thou within this tomb,
From thee, such scenes—thou stintless, lavish Giver,
Tallying the gifts of Earth—large as the Earth,
Thy name an Earth, with mountains, fields and
    rivers.

Nor by your streams alone, you rivers,
By you, your banks, Connecticut,
By you, and all your teeming life, Old Thames,
By you, Potomac, laving the ground Washington
    trod—by you Patapsco,
You, Hudson—you, endless Mississippi—not by you
    alone,
But to the high seas launch, my thought, his memory.

5

Lo, Soul, by this tomb's lambency,
The darkness of the arrogant standards of the world,
With all its flaunting aims, ambitions, pleasures.

(Old, commonplace, and rusty saws,
The rich, the gay, the supercilious, smiled at long,
Now, piercing to the marrow in my bones,
Fused with each drop my heart's blood jets,
Swim in ineffable meaning.)

Lo, Soul, the sphere requireth, portioneth,
To each his share, his measure,
The moderate to the moderate, the ample to the
    ample.

Lo, Soul, see'st thou not, plain as the sun,
The only real wealth of wealth in generosity,
The only life of life in goodness?


## PIONEERS! O PIONEERS!

1

COME, my tan-faced children,
    Follow well in order, get your weapons ready;
    Have you your pistols? have you your sharp
edged axes?
    Pioneers! O pioneers!


2

For we cannot tarry here,
We must march my darlings, we must bear the
    brunt of danger,
We, the youthful sinewy races, all the rest on us
    depend,
        Pioneers! O pioneers!

### 3

O you youths, western youths,
So impatient, full of action, full of manly pride and
    friendship,
Plain I see you, western youths, see you tramping
    with the foremost,
        Pioneers! O pioneers!

### 4

Have the elder races halted?
Do they droop and end their lesson, wearied, over
    there beyond the seas?
We take up the task eternal, and the burden, and
    the lesson,
        Pioneers! O pioneers!

### 5

All the past we leave behind;
We debouch upon a newer, mightier world, varied
    world,
Fresh and strong the world we seize, world of labor
    and the march,
        Pioneers! O pioneers!

### 6

We detachments steady throwing,
Down the edges, through the passes, up the moun-
    tains steep,
Conquering, holding, daring, venturing, as we go,
    the unknown ways,
        Pioneers! O pioneers!

### 7

We primeval forests felling,
We the rivers stemming, vexing we, and piercing
    deep the mines within;

We the surface broad surveying, we the virgin soil
    upheaving,
        Pioneers! O pioneers!

8

Colorado men are we,
From the peaks gigantic, from the great sierras and
    the high plateaus,
From the mine and from the gully, from the hunting
    trail we come,
        Pioneers! O pioneers!

9

From Nebraska, from Arkansas,
Central inland race are we, from Missouri, with the
    continental blood intervein'd;
All the hands of comrades clasping, all the Southern,
    all the Northern,
        Pioneers! O pioneers!

10

O resistless, restless race!
O beloved race in all! O my breast aches with ten-
    der love for all!
O I mourn and yet exult—I am rapt with love for
    all,
        Pioneers! O pioneers!

11

Raise the mighty mother mistress,
Waving high the delicate mistress, over all the starry
    mistress, (bend your heads all,)
Raise the fang'd and warlike mistress, stern, im-
    passive, weapon'd mistress,
        Pioneers! O pioneers!

12

See, my children, resolute children,
By those swarms upon our rear, we must never yield
or falter,
Ages back in ghostly millions, frowning there behind
us urging,
　　　Pioneers! O pioneers!

13

On and on, the compact ranks,
With accessions ever waiting, with the places of the
dead quickly fill'd,
Through the battle, through defeat, moving yet and
never stopping,
　　　Pioneers! O pioneers!

14

O to die advancing on!
Are there some of us to droop and die? has the hour
come?
Then upon the march we fittest die, soon and sure
the gap is fill'd,
　　　Pioneers! O pioneers!

15

All the pulses of the world,
Falling in, they beat for us, with the western move-
ment beat;
Holding single or together, steady moving, to the
front, all for us,
　　　Pioneers! O pioneers!

16

Life's involv'd and varied pageants,
All the forms and shows, all the workmen at their
work,

All the seamen and the landsmen, all the masters
    with their slaves,
        Pioneers! O pioneers!

## 17

All the hapless silent lovers,
All the prisoners in the prisons, all the righteous and
    the wicked,
All the joyous, all the sorrowing, all the living, all
    the dying,
        Pioneers! O pioneers!

## 18

I too with my soul and body,
We, a curious trio, picking, wandering on our way,
Through these shores, amid the shadows, with the
    apparitions pressing,
        Pioneers! O pioneers!

## 19

Lo! the darting bowling orb!
Lo! the brother orbs around! all the clustering suns
    and planets;
All the dazzling days, all the mystic nights with
    dreams,
        Pioneers! O pioneers!

## 20

These are of us, they are with us,
All for primal needed work, while the followers there
    in embryo wait behind,
We to-day's procession heading, we the route for
    travel clearing,
        Pioneers! O pioneers!

21

O you daughters of the west!
O you young and elder daughters! O you mothers
    and you wives!
Never must you be divided, in our ranks you move
    united,
        Pioneers! O pioneers!

22

Minstrels latent on the prairies!
(Shrouded bards of other lands! you may sleep—you
    have done your work;)
Soon I hear you coming warbling, soon you rise
    and tramp amid us,
        Pioneers! O pioneers!

23

Not for delectations sweet;
Not the cushion and the slipper, not the peaceful
    and the studious;
Not the riches safe and palling, not for us the tame
    enjoyment,
        Pioneers! O pioneers!

24

Do the feasters gluttonous feast?
Do the corpulent sleepers sleep? have they lock'd
    and bolted doors?
Still be ours the diet hard, and the blanket on the
    ground,
        Pioneers! O pioneers!

25

Has the night descended?
Was the road of late so toilsome? did we stop dis-
    couraged, nodding on our way?

Yet a passing hour I yield you, in your tracks to
    pause oblivious,
        Pioneers! O pioneers!


26

Till with sound of trumpet,
Far, far off the day-break call—hark! how loud and
    clear I hear it wind;
Swift! to the head of the army!—swift! spring to
    your places,
        Pioneers! O pioneers.


## SONG OF THE EXPOSITION

### 1

AFTER all, not to create only, or found only,
    But to bring, perhaps from afar, what is already
        founded,
To give it our own identity, average, limitless, free;
To fill the gross, the torpid bulk with vital religious
    fire;
Not to repel or destroy, so much as accept, fuse,
    rehabilitate;
To obey, as well as command—to follow, more than
    to lead;
These also are the lessons of our New World;
—While how little the New, after all—how much the
    Old, Old World!

Long, long, long, has the grass been growing,
Long and long has the rain been falling,
Long has the globe been rolling round.

2

Come, Muse, migrate from Greece and Ionia;
Cross out, please, those immensely overpaid accounts,
That matter of Troy, and Achilles' wrath, and Eneas',
  Odysseus' wanderings;
Placard "*Removed*" and "*To Let*" on the rocks of
  your snowy Parnassus;
Repeat at Jerusalem—place the notice high on Jaffa's
  gate, and on Mount Moriah;
The same on the walls of your Gothic European
  Cathedrals, and German, French and Spanish
  Castles;
For know a better, fresher, busier sphere—a wide,
  untried domain awaits, demands you.


3

Responsive to our summons,
Or rather to her long-nurs'd inclination,
Join'd with an irresistible, natural gravitation,
She comes! this famous Female—as was indeed to be
  expected;
(For who, so-ever youthful, 'cute and handsome,
  would wish to stay in mansions such as those,
When offer'd quarters with all the modern improve-
  ments,
With all the fun that 's going—and all the best
  society?)


She comes! I hear the rustling of her gown;
I scent the odor of her breath's delicious fragrance;
I mark her step divine—her curious eyes a-turning,
  rolling,
Upon this very scene.

The Dame of Dames! can I believe, then,
Those ancient temples classic, and castles strong and
  feudalistic, could none of them restrain her?
Nor shades of Virgil and Dante—nor myriad mem-
  ories, poems, old associations, magnetize and hold
  on to her?
But that she 's left them all—and *here?*


Yes, if you will allow me to say so,
I, my friends, if you do not, can plainly see Her,
The same Undying Soul of Earth's, activity's,
  beauty's, heroism's Expression,
Out from her evolutions hither come—submerged
  the strata of her former themes,
Hidden and cover'd by to-day's—foundation of to-
  day's;
Ended, deceas'd, through time, her voice by Castaly's
  fountain;
Silent through time the broken-lipp'd Sphynx in
  Egypt—silent those century-baffling tombs;
Closed for aye the epics of Asia's, Europe's helmeted
  warriors;
Calliope's call for ever closed—Clio, Melpomene,
  Thalia closed and dead;
Seal'd the stately rhythmus of Una and Oriana—
  ended the quest of the Holy Graal;
Jerusalem a handful of ashes blown by the wind—
  extinct;
The Crusaders' streams of shadowy, midnight troops,
  sped with the sunrise;
Amadis, Tancred, utterly gone—Charlemagne, Ro-
  land, Oliver gone,
Palmerin, ogre, departed—vanish'd the turrets that
  Usk reflected,
Arthur vanish'd with all his knights—Merlin and
  Lancelot and Galahad—all gone—dissolv'd utterly,
  like an exhalation;

Pass'd! pass'd! for us, for ever pass'd! that once so
mighty World—now void, inanimate, phantom
World!
Embroider'd, dazzling World! with all its gorgeous
legends, myths,
Its kings and barons proud—its priests, and warlike
lords, and courtly dames;
Pass'd to its charnel vault—laid on the shelf—
coffin'd, with Crown and Armor on,
Blazon'd with Shakspeare's purple page,
And dirged by Tennyson's sweet sad rhyme.

I say I see, my friends, if you do not, the Animus of
all that World,
Escaped, bequeath'd, vital, fugacious as ever, leav-
ing those dead remains, and now this spot ap-
proaching, filling;
—And I can hear what maybe you do not—a terrible
æsthetical commotion,
With howling, desperate gulp of "flower" and
"bower,"
With "Sonnet to Matilda's Eyebrow" quite, quite
frantic;
With gushing, sentimental reading circles turn'd to
ice or stone;
With many a squeak, (in metre choice,) from Bos-
ton, New York, Philadelphia, London;
As she, the illustrious Emigré, (having, it is true, in
her day, although the same, changed, journey'd
considerable,)
Making directly for this rendezvous—vigorously
clearing a path for herself—striding through the
confusion,
By thud of machinery and shrill steam-whistle un-
dismay'd,
Bluff'd not a bit by drain-pipe, gasometers, artificial
fertilizers,

Smiling and pleased, with palpable intent to stay,
She's here, install'd amid the kitchen ware!


### 4

But hold—don't I forget my manners?
To introduce the Stranger (what else indeed have I
    come for?) to thee, Columbia:
In Liberty's name, welcome, Immortal! clasp hands,
And ever henceforth Sisters dear be both.

Fear not, O Muse! truly new ways and days receive,
    surround you,
(I candidly confess, a queer, queer race, of novel
    fashion,)
And yet the same old human race—the same within,
    without,
Faces and hearts the same—feelings the same—
    yearnings the same,
The same old love—beauty and use the same.


### 5

We do not blame thee, Elder World—nor separate
    ourselves from thee:
(Would the Son separate himself from the Father?)
Looking back on thee—seeing thee to thy duties,
    grandeurs, through past ages bending, building,
We build to ours to-day.

Mightier than Egypt's tombs,
Fairer than Grecia's, Roma's temples,
Prouder than Milan's statued, spired Cathedral,
More picturesque than Rhenish castle-keeps,
We plan, even now, to raise, beyond them all,
Thy great Cathedral, sacred Industry—no tomb,
A Keep for life for practical Invention.

As in a waking vision,
E'en while I chant, I see it rise—I scan and prophesy
    outside and in,
Its manifold ensemble.

6

Around a Palace,
Loftier, fairer, ampler than any yet,
Earth's modern Wonder, History's Seven outstrip-
    ping,
High rising tier on tier, with glass and iron façades.

Gladdening the sun and sky—enhued in cheerfulest
    hues,
Bronze, lilac, robin's-egg, marine and crimson,
Over whose golden roof shall flaunt, beneath thy
    banner, Freedom,
The banners of The States, the flags of every land,
A brood of lofty, fair, but lesser Palaces shall cluster.

Somewhere within the walls of all,
Shall all that forwards perfect human life be started,
Tried, taught, advanced, visibly exhibited.

Here shall you trace in flowing operation,
In every state of practical, busy movement,
The rills of Civilization.

Materials here, under your eye, shall change their
    shape, as if by magic;
The cotton shall be pick'd almost in the very field,
Shall be dried, clean'd, ginn'd, baled, spun into
    thread and cloth, before you:
You shall see hands at work at all the old processes,
    and all the new ones;
You shall see the various grains, and how flour is
    made, and then bread baked by the bakers;

You shall see the crude ores of California and Nevada
   passing on and on till they become bullion;
You shall watch how the printer sets type, and learn
   what a composing stick is;
You shall mark, in amazement, the Hoe press whirl-
   ing its cylinders, shedding the printed leaves steady
   and fast:
The photograph, model, watch, pin, nail, shall be
   created before you.

In large calm halls, a stately Museum shall teach
   you the infinite, solemn lessons of Minerals;
In another, woods, plants, Vegetation shall be illus-
   trated—in another Animals, animal life and de-
   velopment.

One stately house shall be the Music House;
Others for other Arts—Learning, the Sciences, shall
   all be here;
None shall be slighted—none but shall here be hon-
   or'd, help'd, exampled.


7

This, this and these, America, shall be *your* Pyra-
   mids and Obelisks,
Your Alexandrian Pharos, gardens of Babylon,
Your temple at Olympia.

The male and female many laboring not,
Shall ever here confront the laboring many,
With precious benefits to both—glory to all,
To thee, America—and thee, Eternal Muse.

And here shall ye inhabit, Powerful Matrons!
In your vast state, vaster than all the old;
Echoed through long, long centuries to come,

To sound of different, prouder songs, with stronger
  themes,
Practical, peaceful life—the people's life—the People
  themselves,
Lifted, illumin'd, bathed in peace—elate, secure in
  peace.

### 8

Away with themes of war! away with War itself!
Hence from my shuddering sight, to never more
  return, that show of blacken'd, mutilated corpses!
That hell unpent, and raid of blood—fit for wild
  tigers, or for lop-tongued wolves—not reasoning
  men!
And in its stead speed Industry's campaigns!
With thy undaunted armies, Engineering!
Thy pennants, Labor, loosen'd to the breeze!
Thy bugles sounding loud and clear!

Away with old romance!
Away with novels, plots, and plays of foreign courts!
Away with love-verses, sugar'd in rhyme—the in-
  trigues, amours of idlers,
Fitted for only banquets of the night, where dancers
  to late music slide;
The unhealthy pleasures, extravagant dissipations
  of the few,
With perfumes, heat and wine, beneath the dazzling
  chandeliers.

### 9

To you, ye Reverent, sane Sisters,
To this resplendent day, the present scene,
These eyes and ears that like some broad parterre
  bloom up around, before me,
I raise a voice for far superber themes for poets and
  for Art,

To exalt the present and the real,
To teach the average man the glory of his daily walk
    and trade,
To sing, in songs, how exercise and chemical life are
    never to be baffled;
Boldly to thee, America, to-day! and thee, Immortal
    Muse!
To practical, manual work, for each and all—to
    plough, hoe, dig,
To plant and tend the tree, the berry, the vegetables,
    flowers,
For every man to see to it that he really do some-
    thing—for every woman too;
To use the hammer, and the saw, (rip or cross-cut,)
To cultivate a turn for carpentering, plastering,
    painting,
To work as tailor, tailoress, nurse, hostler, porter,
To invent a little—something ingenious—to aid the
    washing, cooking, cleaning,
And hold it no disgrace to take a hand at them them-
    selves.

I say I bring thee, Muse, to-day and here,
All occupations, duties broad and close,
Toil, healthy toil and sweat, endless, without cessa-
    tion,
The old, old general burdens, interests, joys,
The family, parentage, childhood, husband and wife,
The house-comforts—the house itself, and all its be-
    longings,
Food and its preservations—chemistry applied to it;
Whatever forms the average, strong, complete,
    sweet-blooded Man or Woman—the perfect,
    longeve Personality,
And helps its present life to health and happiness—
    and shapes its Soul,
For the eternal Real Life to come.

With latest materials, works,
Steam-power, the great Express lines, gas, petro-
leum,
These triumphs of our time, the Atlantic's delicate
cable,
The Pacific Railroad, the Suez canal, the Mont
Cenis tunnel;
Science advanced, in grandeur and reality, analyzing
every thing,
This world all spann'd with iron rails—with lines of
steamships threading every sea,
Our own Rondure, the current globe I bring.

10

And thou, high-towering One—America!
Thy swarm of offspring towering high—yet higher
thee, above all towering,
With Victory on thy left, and at thy right hand Law;
Thou Union, holding all—fusing, absorbing, tolerat-
ing all,
Thee, ever thee, I bring.

Thou—also thou, a world!
With all thy wide geographies, manifold, different,
distant,
Rounding by thee in One—one common orbic
language,
One common indivisible destiny and Union.

11

And by the spells which ye vouchsafe,
To those, your ministers in earnest,
I here personify and call my themes,
To make them pass before ye.

Behold, America! (And thou, ineffable Guest and
    Sister!)
For thee come trooping up thy waters and thy lands:
Behold! thy fields and farms, thy far-off woods and
    mountains,
As in procession coming.

Behold! the sea itself!
And on its limitless, heaving breast, thy ships:
See! where their white sails, bellying in the wind,
    speckle the green and blue!
See! thy steamers coming and going, steaming in or
    out of port!
See! dusky and undulating, their long pennants of
    smoke!

Behold, in Oregon, far in the north and west,
Or in Maine, far in the north and east, thy cheerful
    axemen,
Wielding all day their axes!

Behold, on the lakes, thy pilots at their wheels—thy
    oarsmen!
Behold how the ash writhes under those muscular
    arms!

There by the furnace, and there by the anvil,
Behold thy sturdy blacksmiths, swinging their
    sledges;
Overhand so steady—overhand they turn and fall,
    with joyous clank,
Like a tumult of laughter.

Behold! (for still the procession moves,)
Behold, Mother of All, thy countless sailors, boat-
    men, coasters!

137

The myriads of thy young and old mechanics!
Mark—mark the spirit of invention everywhere—
    thy rapid patents,
Thy continual workshops, foundries, risen or rising;
See, from their chimneys, how the tall flame-fires
    stream!


Mark, thy interminable farms, North, South,
Thy wealthy Daughter-States, Eastern, and West-
    ern,
The varied products of Ohio, Pennsylvania, Mis-
    souri, Georgia, Texas, and the rest;
Thy limitless crops—grass, wheat, sugar, corn, rice,
    hemp, hops,
Thy barns all fill'd—thy endless freight-trains, and
    thy bulging store-houses,
The grapes that ripen on thy vines—the apples in
    thy orchards,
Thy incalculable lumber, beef, pork, potatoes—thy
    coal—thy gold and silver,
The inexhaustible iron in thy mines.



12

All thine, O sacred Union!
Ship, farm, shop, barns, factories, mines,
City and State—North, South, item and aggregate,
We dedicate, dread Mother, all to thee!

Protectress absolute, thou! Bulwark of all!
For well we know that while thou givest each and
    all, (generous as God,)
Without thee, neither all nor each, nor land, home,
Ship, nor mine—nor any here, this day, secure,
Nor aught, nor any day secure.

## 13

And thou, thy Emblem, waving over all!
Delicate beauty! a word to thee, (it may be salu-
tary;)
Remember, thou hast not always been, as here to-
day, so comfortably ensovereign'd;
In other scenes than these have I observ'd thee,
flag;
Not quite so trim and whole, and freshly blooming,
in folds of stainless silk;
But I have seen thee, bunting, to tatters torn, upon
thy splinter'd staff,
Or clutch'd to some young color-bearer's breast,
with desperate hands,
Savagely struggled for, for life or death—fought over
long,
'Mid cannon's thunder-crash, and many a curse, and
groan and yell—and rifle-volleys cracking sharp,
And moving masses, as wild demons surging—and
lives as nothing risk'd,
For thy mere remnant, grimed with dirt and smoke,
and sopp'd in blood;
For sake of that, my beauty—and that thou might'st
dally, as now, secure up there,
Many a good man have I seen go under.

## 14

Now here, and these, and hence, in peace all thine,
O Flag!
And here, and hence, for thee, O universal Muse!
and thou for them!
And here and hence, O Union, all the work and
workmen thine!
The poets, women, sailors, soldiers, farmers, miners,
students thine!

None separate from Thee—henceforth one only, we
and Thou;
(For the blood of the children—what is it only the
blood Maternal?
And lives and works—what are they all at last
except the roads to Faith and Death?)

While we rehearse our measureless wealth, it is for
thee, dear Mother!
We own it all and several to-day indissoluble in
Thee;
—Think not our chant, our show, merely for prod-
ucts gross, or lucre—it is for Thee, the Soul, elec-
tric, spiritual!
Our farms, inventions, crops, we own in Thee!
Cities and States in Thee!
Our freedom all in Thee! our very lives in Thee!

## AS A STRONG BIRD ON PINIONS FREE

I

AS a strong bird on pinions free,
Joyous, the amplest spaces heavenward cleaving,
Such be the thought I'd think to-day of thee,
America,
Such be the recitative I'd bring to-day for thee.

The conceits of the poets of other lands I bring thee
not,
Nor the compliments that have served their turn so
long,
Nor rhyme—nor the classics—nor perfume of
foreign court, or indoor library;
But an odor I'd bring to-day as from forests of pine in
the north, in Maine—or breath of an Illinois prairie,
With open airs of Virginia, or Georgia, or Tennessee
—or from Texas uplands, or Florida's glades,
With presentment of Yellowstone's scenes, or Yose-
mite;
And murmuring under, pervading all, I'd bring the
rustling sea-sound,
That endlessly sounds from the two great seas of
the world.

And for thy subtler sense, subtler refrains, O Union!
Preludes of intellect tallying these and thee—mind-
formulas fitted for thee—real, and sane, and large
as these and thee;
Thou, mounting higher, diving deeper than we knew
—thou transcendental Union!
By thee Fact to be justified—blended with Thought;
Thought of Man justified—blended with God:
Through thy Idea—lo! the immortal Reality!
Through thy Reality—lo! the immortal Idea!

2

Brain of the New World! what a task is thine!
To formulate the Modern. . . . Out of the
    peerless grandeur of the modern,
Out of Thyself—comprising Science—to recast
    Poems, Churches, Art,
(Recast—may-be discard them, end them—May-be
    their work is done—who knows?)
By vision, hand, conception, on the background of
    the mighty past, the dead,
To limn, with absolute faith, the mighty living
    present.


(And yet, thou living, present brain! heir of the
    dead, the Old World brain!
Thou that lay folded, like an unborn babe, within
    its folds so long!
Thou carefully prepared by it so long!—haply thou
    but unfoldest it—only maturest it;
It to eventuate in thee—the essence of the by-gone
    time contain'd in thee;
Its poems, churches, arts, unwitting to themselves,
    destined with reference to thee,
The fruit of all the Old, ripening to-day in thee.)


3

Sail—sail thy best, ship of Democracy!
Of value is thy freight—'tis not the Present only,
The Past is also stored in thee!
Thou holdest not the venture of thyself alone—not
    of thy western continent alone;
Earth's *résumé* entire floats on thy keel, O ship—is
    steadied by thy spars;
With thee Time voyages in trust—the antecedent
    nations sink or swim with thee;

With all their ancient struggles, martyrs, heroes,
    epics, wars, thou bear'st the other continents;
Theirs, theirs as much as thine, the destination-port
    triumphant:
—Steer, steer with good strong hand and wary eye,
    O helmsman—thou carryest great companions,
Venerable, priestly Asia sails this day with thee,
And royal, feudal Europe sails with thee.

4

Beautiful World of new, superber Birth, that rises
    to my eyes,
Like a limitless golden cloud, filling the western sky;
Emblem of general Maternity, lifted above all;
Sacred shape of the bearer of daughters and sons;
Out of thy teeming womb, thy giant babes in cease-
    less procession issuing,
Acceding from such gestation, taking and giving con-
    tinual strength and life;
World of the Real! world of the twain in one!
World of the Soul—born by the world of the real
    alone—led to identity, body, by it alone;
Yet in beginning only—incalculable masses of com-
    posite, precious materials,
By history's cycles forwarded—by every nation,
    language, hither sent,
Ready, collected here—a freer, vast, electric World,
    to be constructed here,
(The true New World—the world of orbic Science,
    Morals, Literatures to come,)
Thou Wonder World, yet undefined, unform'd—
    neither do I define thee;
How can I pierce the impenetrable blank of the
    future?
I feel thy ominous greatness, evil as well as good;
I watch thee, advancing, absorbing the present,
    transcending the past;

I see thy light lighting and thy shadow shadowing, as
    if the entire globe;
But I do not undertake to define thee—hardly to
    comprehend thee;
I but thee name—thee prophecy—as now!
I merely thee ejaculate!


Thee in thy future;
Thee in thy only permanent life, career—thy own
    unloosen'd mind—thy soaring spirit;
Thee as another equally needed sun, America—
    radiant, ablaze, swift-moving, fructifying all;
Thee! risen in thy potent cheerfulness and joy—thy
    endless, great hilarity!
(Scattering for good the cloud that hung so long—
    that weigh'd so long upon the mind of man,
The doubt, suspicion, dread, of gradual, certain de-
    cadence of man;)
Thee in thy larger, saner breeds of Female, Male—
    thee in thy athletes, moral, spiritual, South,
    North, West, East,
(To thy immortal breasts, Mother of All, thy every
    daughter, son, endear'd alike, forever equal;)
Thee in thy own musicians, singers, artists, unborn
    yet, but certain;
Thee in thy moral wealth and civilization (until
    which thy proudest material wealth and civiliza-
    tion must remain in vain;)
Thee in thy all-supplying, all-enclosing Worship—
    thee in no single bible, saviour, merely,
Thy saviours countless, latent within thyself—thy
    bibles incessant, within thyself, equal to any,
    divine as any;
Thee in an education grown of thee—in teachers,
    studies, students, born of thee;
Thee in thy democratic fêtes, en masse—thy high
    original festivals, operas, lecturers, preachers;

Thee in thy ultimata, (the preparations only now
  completed—the edifice on sure foundations tied,)
Thee in thy pinnacles, intellect, thought—thy top-
  most rational joys—thy love, and godlike aspira-
  tion,
In thy resplendent coming literati—thy full-lung'd
  orators—thy sacerdotal bards—kosmic savans,
These! these in thee, (certain to come,) to-day I
  prophecy.

5

Land tolerating all—accepting all—not for the good
  alone—all good for thee;
Land in the realms of God to be a realm unto thyself;
Under the rule of God to be a rule unto thyself.


(Lo! where arise three peerless stars,
To be thy natal stars, my country—Ensemble—
  Evolution—Freedom,
Set in the sky of Law.)


Land of unprecedented faith—God's faith!
Thy soil, thy very subsoil, all upheav'd;
The general inner earth, so long, so sedulously draped
  over, now and hence for what it is, boldly laid
  bare,
Open'd by thee to heaven's light, for benefit or bale.


Not for success alone;
Not to fair-sail unintermitted always;
The storm shall dash thy face—the murk of war, and
  worse than war, shall cover thee all over;
(Wert capable of war—its tug and trials?  Be capable
  of peace, its trials;
For the tug and mortal strain of nations come at last
  in peace—not war;)

In many a smiling mask death shall approach, be-
  guiling thee—thou in disease shalt swelter;
The livid cancer spread its hideous claws, clinging
  upon thy breasts, seeking to strike thee deep
  within;
Consumption of the worst—moral consumption—
  shall rouge thy face with hectic:
But thou shalt face thy fortunes, thy diseases, and
  surmount them all,
Whatever they are to-day, and whatever through
  time they may be,
They each and all shall lift, and pass away, and cease
  from thee;
While thou, Time's spirals rounding—out of thy-
  self, thyself still extricating, fusing,
Equable, natural, mystical Union thou—(the mortal
  with immortal blent,)
Shalt soar toward the fulfilment of the future—the
  spirit of the body and the mind,
The Soul—its destinies.

The Soul, its destinies—the real real,
(Purport of all these apparitions of the real;)
In thee, America, the Soul, its destinies;
Thou globe of globes! thou wonder nebulous!
By many a throe of heat and cold convuls'd—(by
  these thyself solidifying;)
Thou mental, moral orb! thou New, indeed new,
  Spiritual World!
The Present holds thee not—for such vast growth as
  thine—for such unparallel'd flight as thine,
The Future only holds thee, and can hold thee.

## THIS MOMENT, YEARNING AND THOUGHTFUL

*THIS moment yearning and thoughtful, sitting
   alone,
   It seems to me there are other men in other lands,
   yearning and thoughtful;
It seems to me I can look over and behold them, in
   Germany, Italy, France, Spain—or far, far away,
   in China, or in Russia or India—talking other
   dialects;
And it seems to me if I could know those men, I should
   become attached to them, as I do to men in my own
   lands;
O I know we should be brethren and lovers,
I know I should be happy with them.*

## PRAYER OF COLUMBUS

It was near the close of his indomitable and pious life—on his last voyage when nearly 70 years of age—that Columbus, to save his two remaining ships from foundering in the Caribbean Sea in a terrible storm, had to run them ashore on the Island of Jamaica—where, laid up for a long and miserable year—1503—he was taken very sick, had several relapses, his men revolted, and death seem'd daily imminent; though he was eventually rescued, and sent home to Spain to die, unrecognized, neglected and in want. . . . . . It is only ask'd, as preparation and atmosphere for the following lines, that the bare authentic facts be recall'd and realized, and nothing contributed by the fancy. See, the Antillean Island, with its florid skies and rich foliage and scenery, the waves beating the solitary sands, and the hulls of the ships in the distance. See, the figure of the great Admiral, walking the beach, as a stage, in this sublimest tragedy—for what tragedy, what poem, so piteous and majestic as the real scene?—and hear him uttering—as his mystical and religious soul surely utter'd, the ideas following—perhaps, in their equivalents, the very words.

A BATTER'D, wreck'd old man,
Thrown on this savage shore, far, far from
home,
Pent by the sea, and dark rebellious brows, twelve
dreary months,
Sore, stiff with many toils, sicken'd, and nigh to
death,
I take my way along the island's edge,
Venting a heavy heart.

I am too full of woe!
Haply, I may not live another day;
I can not rest, O God—I can not eat or drink or
sleep,
Till I put forth myself, my prayer, once more to
Thee,
Breathe, bathe myself once more in Thee—commune
with Thee,
Report myself once more to Thee.

Thou knowest my years entire, my life,
(My long and crowded life of active work—not
adoration merely;)
Thou knowest the prayers and vigils of my youth;

Thou knowest my manhood's solemn and visionary
     meditations;
Thou knowest how, before I commenced, I devoted
     all to come to Thee;
Thou knowest I have in age ratified all those vows,
     and strictly kept them;
Thou knowest I have not once lost nor faith nor
     ecstasy in Thee;
(In shackles, prison'd, in disgrace, repining not,
Accepting all from Thee—as duly come from Thee.)

All my emprises have been fill'd with Thee,
My speculations, plans, begun and carried on in
     thoughts of Thee,
Sailing the deep, or journeying the land for Thee;
Intentions, purports, aspirations mine—leaving re-
     sults to Thee.

O I am sure they really come from Thee!
The urge, the ardor, the unconquerable will,
The potent, felt, interior command, stronger than
     words,
A message from the Heavens, whispering to me even
     in sleep,
These sped me on.

By me, and these, the work so far accomplish'd (for
     what has been, has been;)
By me Earth's elder, cloy'd and stifled lands, un-
     cloy'd, unloos'd;
By me the hemispheres rounded and tied—the un-
     known to the known.

The end I know not—it is all in Thee;
Or small, or great, I know not—haply, what broad
     fields, what lands;
Haply, the brutish, measureless human undergrowth
     I know,

Transplanted there, may rise to stature, knowledge
    worthy Thee;
Haply the swords I know may there indeed be turn'd
    to reaping-tools;
Haply the lifeless cross I know—Europe's dead cross
    —may bud and blossom there.

One effort more—my altar this bleak sand:
That Thou, O God, my life hast lighted,
With ray of light, steady, ineffable, vouchsafed of
    Thee,
(Light rare, untellable—lighting the very light!
Beyond all signs, descriptions, languages!)
For that, O God—be it my latest word—here on my
    knees,
Old, poor, and paralyzed—I thank Thee.

My terminus near,
The clouds already closing in upon me,
The voyage balk'd—the course disputed, lost,
I yield my ships to Thee.

Steersman unseen! henceforth the helms are Thine;
Take Thou command—(what to my petty skill Thy
    navigation?)
My hands, my limbs grow nerveless;
My brain feels rack'd, bewilder'd;
Let the old timbers part—I will not part!
I will cling fast to Thee, O God, though the waves
    buffet me;
Thee, Thee, at least, I know.

Is it the prophet's thought I speak, or am I raving?
What do I know of life? what of myself?
I know not even my own work, past or present;
Dim, ever-shifting guesses of it spread before me,
Of newer, better worlds, their mighty parturition,
Mocking, perplexing me.

And these things I see suddenly—what mean they?
As if some miracle, some hand divine unseal'd my
    eyes,
Shadowy, vast shapes, smile through the air and sky,
And on the distant waves sail countless ships,
And anthems in new tongues I hear saluting me.


## YEARS OF THE MODERN

YEARS of the modern! years of the unperform'd!
    Your horizon rises—I see it parting away for
    more august dramas;
I see not America only—I see not only Liberty's
    nation, but other nations preparing;
I see tremendous entrances and exits—I see new
    combinations—I see the solidarity of races;
I see that force advancing with irresistible power on
    the world's stage;
(Have the old forces, the old wars, played their
    parts? are the acts suitable to them closed?)
I see Freedom, completely arm'd, and victorious, and
    very haughty, with Law on one side, and Peace on
    the other,
A stupendous Trio, all issuing forth against the idea
    of caste;
—What historic denouements are these we so rapidly
    approach?
I see men marching and countermarching by swift
    millions;
I see the frontiers and boundaries of the old aris-
    tocracies broken;
I see the landmarks of European kings removed;
I see this day the People beginning their landmarks,
    (all others give way;)
—Never were such sharp questions ask'd as this day;

Never was average man, his soul, more energetic,
  more like a God;
Lo! how he urges and urges, leaving the masses no
  rest;
His daring foot is on land and sea everywhere—he
  colonizes the Pacific, the archipelagoes;
With the steam-ship, the electric telegraph, the news-
  paper, the wholesale engines of war,
With these, and the world-spreading factories, he
  interlinks all geography, all lands;
—What whispers are these, O lands, running ahead
  of you, passing under the seas?
Are all nations communing? is there going to be but
  one heart to the globe?
Is humanity forming, en-masse?—for lo! tyrants
  tremble, crowns grow dim;
The earth, restive, confronts a new era, perhaps a
  general divine war;
No one knows what will happen next—such portents
  fill the days and nights;
Years prophetical! the space ahead as I walk, as I
  vainly try to pierce it, is full of phantoms;
Unborn deeds, things soon to be, project their shapes
  around me;
This incredible rush and heat—this strange extatic
  fever of dreams, O years!
Your dreams, O year, how they penetrate through
  me! (I know not whether I sleep or wake!)
The perform'd America and Europe grow dim, retir-
  ing in shadow behind me,
The unperform'd, more gigantic than ever, advance,
  advance upon me.

## A BROADWAY PAGEANT

### 1

OVER the western sea, hither from Niphon come,
      Courteous, the swart-cheek'd two-sworded envoys,
Leaning back in their open barouches, bare-headed, impassive,
Ride to-day through Manhattan.

Libertad!
I do not know whether others behold what I behold,
In the procession, along with the nobles of Asia, the errand-bearers,
Bringing up the rear, hovering above, around, or in the ranks marching;
But I will sing you a song of what I behold, Libertad.

### 2

When million-footed Manhattan, unpent, descends to her pavements;
When the thunder-cracking guns arouse me with the proud roar I love;
When the round-mouth'd guns, out of the smoke and smell I love, spit their salutes;
When the fire-flashing guns have fully alerted me—when heaven-clouds canopy my city with a delicate thin haze;
When, gorgeous, the countless straight stems, the forests at the wharves, thicken with colors;
When every ship, richly drest, carries her flag at the peak;
When pennants trail, and street-festoons hang from the windows;
When Broadway is entirely given up to foot-passengers and foot-standers—when the mass is densest;

When the façades of the houses are alive with people
　　—when eyes gaze, riveted, tens of thousands at a
　　time;
When the guests from the islands advance—when the
　　pageant moves forward, visible;
When the summons is made—when the answer that
　　waited thousands of years, answers;
I too, arising, answering, descend to the pavements,
　　merge with the crowd, and gaze with them.


3

Superb-faced Manhattan!
Comrade Americanos!—to us, then, at last, the
　　Orient comes.

To us, my city,
Where our tall-topt marble and iron beauties range
　　on opposite sides—to walk in the space between,
To-day our Antipodes comes.

The Originatress comes,
The nest of languages, the bequeather of poems, the
　　race of eld,
Florid with blood, pensive, rapt with musings, hot
　　with passion,
Sultry with perfume, with ample and flowing gar-
　　ments,
With sunburnt visage, with intense soul and glitter-
　　ing eyes,
The race of Brahma comes!


4

See, my cantabile! these, and more, are flashing to us
　　from the procession;
As it moves, changing, a kaleidoscope divine it
　　moves, changing, before us.

For not the envoys, nor the tann'd Japanee from his
island only;
Lithe and silent, the Hindoo appears—the Asiatic
continent itself appears—the Past, the dead,
The murky night-morning of wonder and fable,
inscrutable,
The envelop'd mysteries, the old and unknown hive-
bees,
The North—the sweltering South—eastern Assyria
—the Hebrews—the Ancient of Ancients,
Vast desolated cities—the gliding Present—all of
these, and more, are in the pageant-procession.

Geography, the world, is in it;
The Great Sea, the brood of islands, Polynesia, the
coast beyond;
The coast you, henceforth, are facing—you Libertad!
from your Western golden shores
The countries there, with their populations—the
millions en-masse, are curiously here;
The swarming market places—the temples, with
idols ranged along the sides, or at the end—bonze,
brahmin, and lama;
The mandarin, farmer, merchant, mechanic, and
fisherman;
The singing-girl and the dancing-girl—the ecstatic
person—the secluded Emperors,
Confucius himself—the great poets and heroes—the
warriors, the castes, all,
Trooping up, crowding from all directions—from the
Altay mountains,
From Thibet—from the four winding and far-flowing
rivers of China,
From the Southern peninsulas, and the demi-con-
tinental islands—from Malaysia;
These, and whatever belongs to them, palpable, show
forth to me, and are seiz'd by me,

And I am seiz'd by them, and friendlily held by
   them,
Till, as here, them all I chant, Libertad! for them-
   selves and for you.

5

For I too, raising my voice, join the ranks of this
   pageant;
I am the chanter—I chant aloud over the pageant;
I chant the world on my Western Sea;
I chant, copious, the islands beyond, thick as stars in
   the sky;
I chant the new empire, grander than any before—
   As in a vision it comes to me;
I chant America, the Mistress—I chant a greater
   supremacy;
I chant, projected, a thousand blooming cities yet, in
   time, on those groups of sea-islands;
I chant my sail-ships and steam-ships threading the
   archipelagoes;
I chant my stars and stripes fluttering in the wind;
I chant commerce opening, the sleep of ages having
   done its work—races, reborn, refresh'd;
Lives, works, resumed—The object I know not—but
   the old, the Asiatic, renew'd, as it must be,
Commencing from this day, surrounded by the world.

6

And you, Libertad of the world!
You shall sit in the middle, well-pois'd, thousands of
   years;
As to-day, from one side, the nobles of Asia come to
   you;
As to-morrow, from the other side, the Queen of
   England sends her eldest son to you.

### 7

The sign is reversing, the orb is enclosed,
The ring is circled, the journey is done;
The box-lid is but perceptibly open'd—nevertheless
the perfume pours copiously out of the whole box.

### 8

Young Libertad!
With the venerable Asia, the all-mother,
Be considerate with her, now and ever, hot Libertad
—for you are all;
Bend your proud neck to the long-off mother, now
sending messages over the archipelagoes to you;
Bend your proud neck low for once, young Libertad.

### 9

Were the children straying westward so long? so
wide the tramping?
Were the precedent dim ages debouching westward
from Paradise so long?
Were the centuries steadily footing it that way, all
the while unknown, for you, for reasons?

They are justified—they are accomplish'd—they
shall now be turn'd the other way also, to travel
toward you thence;
They shall now also march obediently eastward, for
your sake, Libertad.

## FRANCE

### 1

A GREAT year and place;
A harsh, discordant, natal scream out-sound-
ing, to touch the mother's heart closer than
any yet.

I walk'd the shores of my Eastern Sea,
Heard over the waves the little voice,
Saw the divine infant, where she woke, mournfully
    wailing, amid the roar of cannon, curses, shouts,
    crash of falling buildings;
Was not so sick from the blood in the gutters running
    —nor from the single corpses, nor those in heaps,
    nor those borne away in the tumbrils;
Was not so desperate at the battues of death—was
    not so shock'd at the repeated fusillades of the
    guns.

### 2

Pale, silent, stern, what could I say to that long-
    accrued retribution?
Could I wish humanity different?
Could I wish the people made of wood and stone?
Or that there be no justice in destiny or time?

### 3

O Liberty! O mate for me!
Here too the blaze, the grape-shot and the axe, in
    reserve, to fetch them out in case of need;
Here too, though long represt, can never be destroy'd;
Here too could rise at last, murdering and extatic;
Here too demanding full arrears of vengeance.

### 4

Hence I sign this salute over the sea,

And I do not deny that terrible red birth and baptism,

But remember the little voice that I heard wailing—
  and wait with perfect trust, no matter how long;

And from to-day, sad and cogent, I maintain the
  bequeath'd cause, as for all lands,

And I send these words to Paris with my love,

And I guess some chansonniers there will understand
  them,

For I guess there is latent music yet in France—
  floods of it;

O I hear already the bustle of instruments—they
  will soon be drowning all that would interrupt
  them;

O I think the east wind brings a triumphal and free
  march,

It reaches hither—it swells me to joyful madness,

I will run transpose it in words, to justify it,

I will yet sing a song for you, MA FEMME.

## TO A FOIL'D EUROPEAN REVOLUTIONAIRE

1

COURAGE yet! my brother or my sister!
Keep on! Liberty is to be subserv'd, whatever
  occurs;
That is nothing, that is quell'd by one or two failures,
  or any number of failures,
Or by the indifference or ingratitude of the people,
  or by any unfaithfulness,
Or the show of the tushes of power, soldiers, cannon,
  penal statutes.

Revolt! and still revolt! revolt!
What we believe in waits latent forever through all
  the continents, and all the islands and archipelagos
  of the sea;
What we believe in invites no one, promises nothing,
  sits in calmness and light, is positive and com-
  posed, knows no discouragement,
Waiting patiently, waiting its time.

(Not songs of loyalty alone are these,
But songs of insurrection also;
For I am the sworn poet of every dauntless rebel, the
  world over,
And he going with me leaves peace and routine be-
  hind him,
And stakes his life, to be lost at any moment.)

2

Revolt! and the downfall of tyrants!
The battle rages with many a loud alarm, and fre-
  quent advance and retreat,
The infidel triumphs—or supposes he triumphs,
Then the prison, scaffold, garrote, hand-cuffs, iron
  necklace and anklet, lead-balls, do their work,

The named and unnamed heroes pass to other spheres,
The great speakers and writers are exiled—they lie
    sick in distant lands,
The cause is asleep—the strongest throats are still,
    choked with their own blood,
The young men droop their eyelashes toward the
    ground when they meet;
—But for all this, liberty has not gone out of the
    place, nor the infidel enter'd into full possession.

When liberty goes out of a place, it is not the first to
    go, nor the second or third to go,
It waits for all the rest to go—it is the last.

When there are no more memories of heroes and
    martyrs,
And when all life, and all the souls of men and
    women are discharged from any part of the earth,
Then only shall liberty, or the idea of liberty, be dis-
    charged from that part of the earth,
And the infidel come into full possession.


3
Then courage! European revolter! revoltress!
For, till all ceases, neither must you cease.

I do not know what you are for, (I do not know what
    I am for myself, nor what anything is for,)
But I will search carefully for it even in being foil'd,
In defeat, poverty, misconception, imprisonment—
    for they too are great.

Revolt! and the bullet for tyrants!
Did we think victory great?
So it is—But now it seems to me, when it cannot be
    help'd, that defeat is great,
And that death and dismay are great.

## EUROPE

### 1

SUDDENLY, out of its stale and drowsy lair, the
    lair of slaves,
    Like lightning it le'pt forth, half startled at itself,
Its feet upon the ashes and the rags—its hands tight
    to the throats of kings.

O hope and faith!
O aching close of exiled patriots' lives!
O many a sicken'd heart!
Turn back unto this day, and make yourselves afresh.

And you, paid to defile the People! you liars, mark!
Not for numberless agonies, murders, lusts,
For court thieving in its manifold mean forms, worm-
    ing from his simplicity the poor man's wages,
For many a promise sworn by royal lips, and broken,
    and laugh'd at in the breaking,
Then in their power, not for all these, did the blows
    strike revenge, or the heads of the nobles fall;
The People scorn'd the ferocity of kings.

### 2

But the sweetness of mercy brew'd bitter destruction,
    and the frighten'd monarchs come back;
Each comes in state, with his train—hangman,
    priest, taxgatherer,
Soldier, lawyer, lord, jailer, and sycophant.

Yet behind all, lowering, stealing—lo, a Shape,
Vague as the night, draped interminably, head, front
    and form, in scarlet folds,
Whose face and eyes none may see,
Out of its robes only this—the red robes, lifted by the
    arm,

One finger, crook'd, pointed high over the top, like
the head of a snake appears.

### 3

Meanwhile, corpses lie in new-made graves—bloody
corpses of young men;
The rope of the gibbet hangs heavily, the bullets of
princes are flying, the creatures of power laugh
aloud,
And all these things bear fruits—and they are good.

Those corpses of young men,
Those martyrs that hang from the gibbets—those
hearts pierc'd by the gray lead,
Cold and motionless as they seem, live elsewhere with
unslaughter'd vitality.

They live in other young men, O kings!
They live in brothers, again ready to defy you!
They were purified by death—they were taught and
exalted.

Not a grave of the murder'd for freedom, but grows
seed for freedom, in its turn to bear seed,
Which the winds carry afar and re-sow, and the rains
and the snows nourish.

Not a disembodied spirit can the weapons of tyrants
let loose,
But it stalks invisibly over the earth, whispering,
counseling, cautioning.

### 4

Liberty! let others despair of you! I never despair of
you.
Is the house shut?  Is the master away?
Nevertheless, be ready—be not weary of watching;
He will soon return—his messengers come anon.

## SONG FOR ALL SEAS, ALL SHIPS

### 1

TO-DAY a rude brief recitative,
 Of ships sailing the Seas, each with its special
 flag or ship-signal;
Of unnamed heroes in the ships—Of waves spreading
 and spreading, far as the eye can reach;
Of dashing spray, and the winds piping and blowing;
And out of these a chant, for the sailors of all nations,
Fitful, like a surge.

Of Sea-Captains young or old, and the Mates—and
 of all intrepid Sailors;
Of the few, very choice, taciturn, whom fate can
 never surprise, nor death dismay,
Pick'd sparingly, without noise, by thee, old Ocean—
 chosen by thee,
Thou Sea, that pickest and cullest the race, in Time,
 and unitest Nations!
Suckled by thee, old husky Nurse—embodying thee!
Indomitable, untamed as thee.

(Ever the heroes, on water or on land, by ones or twos
 appearing,
Ever the stock preserv'd, and never lost, though
 rare—enough for seed preserv'd.)

### 2

Flaunt out O Sea, your separate flags of nations!
Flaunt out, visible as ever, the various ship-signals!
But do you reserve especially for yourself, and for
 the soul of man, one flag above all the rest,
A spiritual woven Signal, for all nations, emblem of
 man elate above death,

Token of all brave captains, and all intrepid sailors
  and mates,
And all that went down doing their duty;
Reminiscent of them—twined from all intrepid cap-
  tains, young or old;
A pennant universal, subtly waving, all time, o'er all
  brave sailors,
All seas, all ships.


## SPAIN, 1873-'74

OUT of the murk of heaviest clouds,
  Out of the feudal wrecks, and heap'd-up skele-
    tons of kings,
Out of that old entire European debris—the shat-
  ter'd mummeries,
Ruin'd cathedrals, crumble of palaces, tombs of
  priests,
Lo! Freedom's features, fresh, undimm'd, look forth
  —the same immortal face looks forth;
(A glimpse as of thy mother's face, Columbia,
A flash significant as of a sword,
Beaming towards thee.)

Nor think we forget thee, Maternal;
Lag'd'st thou so long?  Shall the clouds close again
  upon thee?
Ah, but thou hast Thyself now appear'd to us—we
  know thee;
Thou hast given us a sure proof, the glimpse of Thy-
  self;
Thou waitest there, as everywhere, thy time.

## O STAR OF FRANCE!

1870-71

### 1

O STAR of France!
    The brightness of thy hope and strength and
        fame,
Like some proud ship that led the fleet so long,
Beseems to-day a wreck, driven by the gale—a mast-
    less hulk;
And 'mid its teeming, madden'd, half-drown'd
    crowds,
Nor helm nor helmsman.

### 2

Dim, smitten star!
Orb not of France alone—pale symbol of my soul, its
    dearest hopes,
The struggle and the daring—rage divine for liberty,
Of aspirations toward the far ideal—enthusiast's
    dreams of brotherhood,
Of terror to the tyrant and the priest.

### 3

Star crucified! by traitors sold!
Star panting o'er a land of death—heroic land!
Strange, passionate, mocking, frivolous land.

Miserable! yet for thy errors, vanities, sins, I will not
    now rebuke thee;
Thy unexampled woes and pangs have quell'd them
    all,
And left thee sacred.

In that amid thy many faults, thou ever aimedest
    highly,
In that thou wouldst not really sell thyself, however
    great the price,
In that thou surely wakedst weeping from thy
    drugg'd sleep,
In that alone, among thy sisters, thou, Giantess,
    didst rend the ones that shamed thee,
In that thou couldst not, wouldst not, wear the usual
    chains,
This cross, thy livid face, thy pierced hands and feet,
The spear thrust in thy side.

### 4

O star! O ship of France, beat back and baffled long!
Bear up, O smitten orb! O ship, continue on!

Sure, as the ship of all, the Earth itself,
Product of deathly fire and turbulent chaos,
Forth from its spasms of fury and its poisons,
Issuing at last in perfect power and beauty,
Onward, beneath the sun, following its course,
So thee, O ship of France!

Finish'd the days, the clouds dispell'd,
The travail o'er, the long-sought extrication,
When lo! reborn, high o'er the European world,
(In gladness, answering thence, as face afar to face,
    reflecting ours, Columbia,)
Again thy star, O France—fair, lustrous star,
In heavenly peace, clearer, more bright than ever,
Shall beam immortal.

## PASSAGE TO INDIA

### 1

SINGING my days,
  Singing the great achievements of the present,
  Singing the strong, light works of engineers,
Our modern wonders, (the antique ponderous Seven
    outvied,)
In the Old World, the east, the Suez canal,
The New by its mighty railroad spann'd,
The seas inlaid with eloquent, gentle wires,
I sound, to commence, the cry, with thee, O soul,
The Past! the Past! the Past!

The Past! the dark, unfathom'd retrospect!
The teeming gulf! the sleepers and the shadows!
The past! the infinite greatness of the past!
For what is the present, after all, but a growth out of
    the past?
(As a projectile, form'd, impell'd, passing a certain
    line, still keeps on,
So the present, utterly form'd, impell'd by the past.)

### 2

Passage, O soul, to India!
Eclaircise the myths Asiatic—the primitive fables.

Not you alone, proud truths of the world!
Nor you alone, ye facts of modern science!
But myths and fables of eld—Asia's, Africa's fables!
The far-darting beams of the spirit!—the unloos'd
    dreams!
The deep diving bibles and legends;
The daring plots of the poets—the elder religions;
—O you temples fairer than lilies, pour'd over by the
    rising sun!

O you fables, spurning the known, eluding the hold of
the known, mounting to heaven!
You lofty and dazzling towers, pinnacled, red as
roses, burnish'd with gold!
Towers of fables immortal, fashion'd from mortal
dreams!
You too I welcome, and fully, the same as the rest;
You too with joy I sing.


3

Passage to India!
Lo, soul! seest thou not God's purpose from the first?
The earth to be spann'd, connected by net-work,
The people to become brothers and sisters,
The races, neighbors, to marry and be given in
marriage,
The oceans to be cross'd, the distant brought near,
The lands to be welded together.

(A worship new, I sing;
You captains, voyagers, explorers, yours!
You engineers! you architects, machinists, yours!
You, not for trade or transportation only,
But in God's name, and for thy sake, O soul.)


4

Passage to India!
Lo, soul, for thee, of tableaus twain,
I see, in one, the Suez canal initiated, open'd,
I see the procession of steamships, the Empress
Eugenie's leading the van;
I mark, from on deck, the strange landscape, the
pure sky, the level sand in the distance;
I pass swiftly the picturesque groups, the workmen
gather'd,
The gigantic dredging machines.

In one, again, different, (yet thine, all thine, O soul,
   the same,)
I see over my own continent the Pacific Railroad,
   surmounting every barrier;
I see continual trains of cars winding along the
   Platte, carrying freight and passengers;
I hear the locomotives rushing and roaring, and the
   shrill steam-whistle,
I hear the echoes reverberate through the grandest
   scenery in the world;
I cross the Laramie plains—I note the rocks in
   grotesque shapes—the buttes;
I see the plentiful larkspur and wild onions—the
   barren, colorless, sage-deserts;
I see in glimpses afar, or towering immediately
   above me, the great mountains—I see the Wind
   River and the Wahsatch mountains;
I see the Monument mountain and the Eagle's Nest
   —I pass the Promontory—I ascend the Nevadas;
I scan the noble Elk mountain, and wind around its
   base;
I see the Humboldt range—I thread the valley and
   cross the river,
I see the clear waters of Lake Tahoe—I see forests
   of majestic pines,
Or, crossing the great desert, the alkaline plains, I
   behold enchanting mirages of waters and meadows;
Marking through these, and after all, in duplicate
   slender lines,
Bridging the three or four thousand miles of land
   travel,
Tying the Eastern to the Western sea,
The road between Europe and Asia.

(Ah Genoese, thy dream! thy dream!
Centuries after thou art laid in thy grave,
The shore thou foundest verifies thy dream!)

5

Passage to India!
Struggles of many a captain—tales of many a sailor
    dead!
Over my mood, stealing and spreading they come,
Like clouds and cloudlets in the unreach'd sky.

Along all history, down the slopes,
As a rivulet running, sinking now, and now again to
    the surface rising,
A ceaseless thought, a varied train—Lo, soul! to
    thee, thy sight, they rise,
The plans, the voyages again, the expeditions:
Again Vasco de Gama sails forth;
Again the knowledge gain'd, the mariner's compass,
Lands found, and nations born—thou born, America,
    (a hemisphere unborn,)
For purpose vast, man's long probation fill'd,
Thou, rondure of the world, at last accomplish'd.

6

O, vast Rondure, swimming in space!
Cover'd all over with visible power and beauty!
Alternate light and day, and the teeming, spiritual
    darkness;
Unspeakable, high processions of sun and moon, and
    countless stars, above;
Below, the manifold grass and waters, animals,
    mountains, trees;
With inscrutable purpose—some hidden, prophetic
    intention;
Now, first, it seems, my thought begins to span thee.

Down from the gardens of Asia, descending, radiat-
    ing,
Adam and Eve appear, then their myriad progeny
    after them,

Wandering, yearning, curious—with restless explorations,
With questionings, baffled, formless, feverish—with never-happy hearts,
With that sad, incessant refrain, *Wherefore, unsatisfied Soul?* and *Whither, O mocking Life?*

Ah, who shall soothe these feverish children?
Who justify these restless explorations?
Who speak the secret of impassive Earth?
Who bind it to us? What is this separate Nature, so unnatural?
What is this Earth, to our affections? (unloving earth, without a throb to answer ours;
Cold earth, the place of graves.)

Yet, soul, be sure the first intent remains—and shall be carried out;
(Perhaps even now the time has arrived.)

After the seas are all cross'd, (as they seem already cross'd,)
After the great captains and engineers have accomplish'd their work,
After the noble inventors—after the scientists, the chemist, the geologist, ethnologist,
Finally shall come the Poet, worthy that name;
The true Son of God shall come, singing his songs.

Then, not your deeds only, O voyagers, O scientists and inventors, shall be justified,
All these hearts, as of fretted children, shall be sooth'd,
All affection shall be fully responded to—the secret shall be told;
All these separations and gaps shall be taken up, and hook'd and link'd together;

The whole Earth—this cold, impassive, voiceless
    Earth, shall be completely justified;
Trinitas divine shall be gloriously accomplish'd and
    compacted by the true Son of God, the poet,
(He shall indeed pass the straits and conquer the
    mountains,
He shall double the Cape of Good Hope to some
    purpose;)
Nature and Man shall be disjoin'd and diffused no
    more,
The true Son of God shall absolutely fuse them.

7

Year at whose open'd, wide-flung door I sing!
Year of the purpose accomplish'd!
Year of the marriage of continents, climates and
    oceans!
(No mere Doge of Venice now, wedding the Adriatic;)
I see, O year, in you, the vast terraqueous globe,
    given, and giving all,
Europe to Asia, Africa join'd, and they to the New
    World;
The lands, geographies, dancing before you, holding
    a festival garland,
As brides and bridegrooms hand in hand.

8

Passage to India!
Cooling airs from Caucasus far, soothing cradle of
    man,
The river Euphrates flowing, the past lit up again.

Lo, soul, the retrospect, brought forward;
The old, most populous, wealthiest of Earth's lands,
The streams of the Indus and the Ganges, and their
    many affluents;

(I, my shores of America walking to-day, behold,
   resuming all,)
The tale of Alexander, on his warlike marches, sud-
   denly dying,
On one side China, and on the other side Persia and
   Arabia,
To the south the great seas, and the Bay of Bengal;
The flowing literatures, tremendous epics, religions,
   castes,
Old occult Brahma, interminably far back—the ten-
   der and junior Buddha,
Central and southern empires, and all their belong-
   ings, possessors,
The wars of Tamerlane, the reign of Aurungzebe,
The traders, rulers, explorers, Moslems, Venetians,
   Byzantium, the Arabs, Portuguese,
The first travelers, famous yet, Marco Polo, Batouta
   the Moor,
Doubts to be solv'd, the map incognita, blanks to be
   fill'd,
The foot of man unstay'd, the hands never at rest,
Thyself, O soul, that will not brook a challenge.


9

The medieval navigators rise before me,
The world of 1492, with its awaken'd enterprise;
Something swelling in humanity now like the sap of
   the earth in spring,
The sunset splendor of chivalry declining.

And who art thou, sad shade?
Gigantic, visionary, thyself a visionary,
With majestic limbs, and pious, beaming eyes,
Spreading around, with every look of thine, a golden
   world,
Enhuing it with gorgeous hues.

As the chief histrion,
Down to the footlights walks, in some great scena,
Dominating the rest, I see the Admiral himself,
(History's type of courage, action, faith;)
Behold him sail from Palos, leading his little fleet;
His voyage behold—his return—his great fame,
His misfortunes, calumniators—behold him a pris-
    oner, chain'd,
Behold his dejection, poverty, death.

(Curious, in time, I stand, noting the efforts of heroes;
Is the deferment long? bitter the slander, poverty,
    death?
Lies the seed unreck'd for centuries in the ground?
    Lo! to God's due occasion,
Uprising in the night, it sprouts, blooms,
And fills the earth with use and beauty.)

10

Passage indeed, O soul, to primal thought!
Not lands and seas alone—thy own clear freshness,
The young maturity of brood and bloom;
To realms of budding bibles.

O soul, repressless, I with thee, and thou with me,
Thy circumnavigation of the world begin;
Of man, the voyage of his mind's return,
To reason's early paradise,
Back, back to wisdom's birth, to innocent intuitions,
Again with fair Creation.

11

O we can wait no longer!
We too take ship, O soul!
Joyous, we too launch out on trackless seas!
Fearless, for unknown shores, on waves of extasy to
    sail,

175

Amid the wafting winds, (thou pressing me to thee,
    I thee to me, O soul,)
Caroling free—singing our song of God,
Chanting our chant of pleasant exploration.

With laugh, and many a kiss,
(Let others deprecate—let others weep for sin, re-
    morse, humiliation;)
O soul, thou pleasest me—I thee.

Ah, more than any priest, O soul, we too believe in
    God;
But with the mystery of God we dare not dally.

O soul, thou pleasest me—I thee;
Sailing these seas, or on the hills, or waking in the
    night,
Thoughts, silent thoughts, of Time, and Space, and
    Death, like waters flowing,
Bear me, indeed, as through the regions infinite,
Whose air I breathe, whose ripples hear—lave me
    all over;
Bathe me, O God, in thee—mounting to thee,
I and my soul to range in range of thee.

O Thou transcendant!
Nameless—the fibre and the breath!
Light of the light—shedding forth universes—thou
    centre on them!
Thou mightier centre of the true, the good, the
    loving!
Thou moral, spiritual fountain! affection's source!
    thou reservoir!
(O pensive soul of me! O thirst unsatisfied! waitest
    not there?
Waitest not haply for us, somewhere there, the
    Comrade perfect?)

Thou pulse! thou motive of the stars, suns, systems,
That, circling, move in order, safe, harmonious,
Athwart the shapeless vastnesses of space!
How should I think—how breathe a single breath—
    how speak—if, out of myself,
I could not launch, to those, superior universes?

Swiftly I shrivel at the thought of God,
At Nature and its wonders, Time and Space and
    Death,
But that I, turning, call to thee, O soul, thou actual
    Me,
And lo! thou gently masterest the orbs,
Thou matest Time, smilest content at Death,
And fillest, swellest full, the vastnesses of Space.

Greater than stars or suns,
Bounding, O soul, thou journeyest forth;
—What love, than thine and ours could wider
    amplify?
What aspirations, wishes, outvie thine and ours, O
    soul?
What dreams of the ideal? what plans of purity, per-
    fection, strength?
What cheerful willingness, for others' sake, to give
    up all?
For others' sake to suffer all?

Reckoning ahead, O soul, when thou, the time
    achiev'd,
(The seas all cross'd, weather'd the capes, the voy-
    age done,)
Surrounded, copest, frontest God, yieldest, the aim
    attain'd,
As, fill'd with friendship, love complete, the Elder
    Brother found,
The Younger melts in fondness in his arms.

12

Passage to more than India!
Are thy wings plumed indeed for such far flights?
O Soul, voyagest thou indeed on voyages like these?
Disportest thou on waters such as these?
Soundest below the Sanscrit and the Vedas?
Then have thy bent unleash'd.

Passage to you, your shores, ye aged fierce enigmas!
Passage to you, to mastership of you, ye strangling
  problems!
You, strew'd with the wrecks of skeletons, that, liv-
  ing, never reach'd you.

13

Passage to more than India!
O secret of the earth and sky!
Of you, O waters of the sea! O winding creeks and
  rivers!
Of you, O woods and fields! Of you, strong moun-
  tains of my land!
Of you, O prairies! Of you, gray rocks!
O morning red! O clouds! O rain and snows!
O day and night, passage to you!

O sun and moon, and all you stars! Sirius and Jupiter!
Passage to you!

Passage—immediate passage! the blood burns in my
  veins!
Away, O soul! hoist instantly the anchor!
Cut the hawsers—haul out—shake out every sail!
Have we not stood here like trees in the ground long
  enough?
Have we not grovell'd here long enough, eating and
  drinking like mere brutes?
Have we not darken'd and dazed ourselves with
  books long enough?

Sail forth! steer for the deep waters only!
Reckless, O soul, exploring, I with thee, and thou
    with me;
For we are bound where mariner has not yet dared
    to go,
And we will risk the ship, ourselves and all.

O my brave soul!
O farther, farther sail!
O daring joy, but safe!  Are they not all the seas of
    God?
O farther, farther, farther sail!


## SO FAR AND SO FAR, AND ON TOWARD
## THE END

SO far, and so far, and on toward the end,
    Singing what is sung in this book, from the irre-
      sistible impulses of me;
But whether I continue beyond this book, to ma-
    turity,
Whether I shall dart forth the true rays, the ones
    that wait unfired,
(Did you think the sun was shining its brightest?
No—it has not yet fully risen;)
Whether I shall complete what is here started,
Whether I shall attain my own height, to justify
    these, yet unfinished,
Whether I shall make THE POEM OF THE NEW
    WORLD, transcending all others—depends, rich
    persons, upon you,
Depends, whoever you are now filling the current
    Presidentiad, upon you,
Upon you, Governor, Mayor, Congressman,
And you, contemporary America.

## SOUVENIRS OF DEMOCRACY

THE business man, the acquirer vast,
　　After assiduous years, surveying results, pre-
　　　　paring for departure,
Devises houses and lands to his children—bequeaths
　　stocks, goods—funds for a school or hospital,
Leaves money to certain companions to buy tokens,
　　souvenirs of gems and gold;
Parceling out with care—And then, to prevent all
　　cavil,
His name to his testament formally signs.

But I, my life surveying,
With nothing to show, to devise, from its idle years,
Nor houses, nor lands—nor tokens of gems or gold
　　for my friends,
Only these Souvenirs of Democracy—In them—in
　　all my songs—behind me leaving,
To You, who ever you are, (bathing, leavening this
　　leaf especially with my breath—pressing on it a
　　moment with my own hands;
—Here! feel how the pulse beats in my wrists!—
　　how my heart's-blood is swelling, contracting!)
I will You, in all, Myself, with promise to never
　　desert you,
To which I sign my name.

## NOT THE PILOT

NOT the pilot has charged himself to bring his
ship into port, though beaten back, and
many times baffled;
Not the path-finder, penetrating inland, weary and
long,
By deserts parch'd, snows-chill'd, rivers wet, per-
severes till he reaches his destination,
More than I have charged myself, heeded or un-
heeded, to compose a free march for These States,
To be exhilarating music to them—a battle-call,
rousing to arms, if need be—years, centuries
hence.


## SO LONG!

I

TO conclude—I announce what comes after me;
I announce mightier offspring, orators, days,
and then, for the present, depart.

I remember I said, before my leaves sprang at all,
I would raise my voice jocund and strong, with
reference to consummations.

When America does what was promis'd,
When there are plentiful athletic bards, inland and
seaboard,
When through These States walk a hundred millions
of superb persons,
When the rest part away for superb persons, and
contribute to them,
When breeds of the most perfect mothers denote
America,
Then to me and mine our due fruition.

I have press'd through in my own right,
I have sung the Body and the Soul—War and Peace
 have I sung,
And the songs of Life and of Birth—and shown that
 there are many births:
I have offer'd my style to every one—I have jour-
 ney'd with confident step;
While my pleasure is yet at the full, I whisper, *So
 long!*
And take the young woman's hand, and the young
 man's hand, for the last time.


2

I announce natural persons to arise;
I announce justice triumphant;
I announce uncompromising liberty and equality;
I announce the justification of candor, and the justi-
 fication of pride.


I announce that the identity of These States is a
 single identity only;
I announce the Union more and more compact, in-
 dissoluble;
I announce splendors and majesties to make all the
 previous politics of the earth insignificant.


I announce adhesiveness—I say it shall be limitless,
 unloosen'd;
I say you shall yet find the friend you were looking
 for.


I announce a man or woman coming—perhaps you
 are the one, (*So long!*)
I announce the great individual, fluid as Nature,
 chaste, affectionate, compassionate, fully armed.

I announce a life that shall be copious, vehement,
 spiritual, bold;
I announce an end that shall lightly and joyfully
 meet its translation;
I announce myriads of youths, beautiful, gigantic,
 sweet-blooded;
I announce a race of splendid and savage old men.


3

O thicker and faster! (*So long!*)
O crowding too close upon me;
I foresee too much—it means more than I thought;
It appears to me I am dying.


Hasten throat, and sound your last!
Salute me—salute the days once more. Peal the
 old cry once more.


Screaming electric, the atmosphere using,
At random glancing, each as I notice absorbing,
Swiftly on, but a little while alighting,
Curious envelop'd messages delivering,
Sparkles hot, seed ethereal, down in the dirt drop-
 ping,
Myself unknowing, my commission obeying, to
 question it never daring,
To ages, and ages yet, the growth of the seed leaving,
To troops out of me, out of the army, the war aris-
 ing—they the tasks I have set promulging,
To women certain whispers of myself bequeathing—
 their affection me more clearly explaining,
To young men my problems offering—no dallier I—
 I the muscle of their brains trying,
So I pass—a little time vocal, visible, contrary;
Afterward, a melodious echo, passionately bent for
 —(death making me really undying;)

The best of me then when no longer visible—for to-
ward that I have been incessantly preparing.

What is there more, that I lag and pause, and crouch
extended with unshut mouth?
Is there a single final farewell?

4

My songs cease—I abandon them;
From behind the screen where I hid I advance per-
sonally, solely to you.

Camerado! This is no book;
Who touches this, touches a man;
(Is it night? Are we here alone?)
It is I you hold, and who holds you;
I spring from the pages into your arms—decease calls
me forth.

O how your fingers drowse me!
Your breath falls around me like dew—your pulse
lulls the tympans of my ears;
I feel immerged from head to foot;
Delicious—enough.

Enough, O deed impromptu and secret!
Enough, O gliding present! Enough, O summ'd-up
past!

5

Dear friend, whoever you are, take this kiss,
I give it especially to you—Do not forget me;
I feel like one who has done work for the day, to
retire awhile;
I receive now again of my many translations—from
my avataras ascending—while others doubtless
await me;

An unknown sphere, more real than I dream'd, more
    direct, darts awakening rays about me—*So long!*
Remember my words—I may again return,
I love you—I depart from materials;
I am as one disembodied, triumphant, dead.


## THANKS IN OLD AGE

THANKS in old age—thanks ere I go,
    For health, the midday sun, the impalpable
    air—for life, mere life,
For precious ever-lingering memories, (of you my
    mother dear—you, father—you, brothers, sisters,
    friends,)
For all my days—not those of peace alone—the days
    of war the same,
For gentle words, caresses, gifts from foreign lands,
For shelter, wine and meat—for sweet appreciation,
(You distant, dim unknown—or young or old—
    countless, unspecified, readers belov'd,
We never met, and ne'er shall meet—and yet our
    souls embrace, long, close and long;)
For beings, groups, love, deeds, words, books—for
    colors, forms,
For all the brave strong men—devoted, hardy men—
    who've forward sprung in freedom's help, all
    years, all lands,
For braver, stronger, more devoted men—(a special
    laurel ere I go, to life's war's chosen ones,
The cannoneers of song and thought—the great artil-
    lerists—the foremost leaders, captains of the soul:)
As soldier from an ended war return'd—As traveler
    out of myriads, to the long procession retro-
    spective,
Thanks—joyful thanks!—a soldier's, traveler's
    thanks.

## THOUGHT

AS they draw to a close,
    Of what underlies the precedent songs—of my
    aims in them;
Of the seed I have sought to plant in them;
Of joy, sweet joy, through many a year, in them;
(For them—for them have I lived—In them my
    work is done;)
Of many an aspiration fond—of many a dream and
    plan,
Of you, O mystery great!—to place on record faith
    in you, O death!
—To compact you, ye parted, diverse lives!
To put rapport the mountains, and rocks, and
    streams,
And the winds of the north, and the forests of oak
    and pine,
With you, O soul of man.

## IN FORMER SONGS

1

IN former songs Pride have I sung, and Love, and
    passionate, joyful Life,
    But here I twine the strands of Patriotism and
    Death.

And now, Life, Pride, Love, Patriotism and Death,
To you, O FREEDOM, purport of all!
(You that elude me most—refusing to be caught in
    songs of mine,)
I offer all to you.

2

'Tis not for nothing, Death,
I sound out you, and words of you, with daring
    tone—embodying you,

In my new Democratic chants—keeping you for a
   close,
For last impregnable retreat—a citadel and tower,
For my last stand—my pealing, final cry.


## LESSONS

THERE are who teach only the sweet lessons of
      peace and safety;
      But I teach lessons of war and death to those
   I love,
That they readily meet invasions, when they come.


## ONE SONG, AMERICA, BEFORE I GO

ONE song, America, before I go,
      I'd sing, o'er all the rest, with trumpet sound,
      For thee—the Future.

I'd sow a seed for thee of endless Nationality;
I'd fashion thy Ensemble, including Body and Soul;
I'd show, away ahead, thy real Union, and how it
   may be accomplish'd.

(The paths to the House I seek to make,
But leave to those to come, the House itself.)

Belief I sing—and Preparation;
As Life and Nature are not great with reference to
   the Present only,
But greater still from what is yet to come,
Out of that formula for Thee I sing.